Praise for
Man Alive

"I've talked to tens of thousands of men who feel beat down and knocked around for bad decisions they've made. Some of these guys feel like such failures they can't even imagine a heavenly Father who loves them unconditionally. To each of these men I say, you need to hear the truth and brother-to-brother encouragement that Patrick Morley delivers in *Man Alive*!"

> —DAVE RAMSEY, *New York Times* best-selling author,
> nationally syndicated radio talk-show host, and founder
> of Financial Peace University

"Most men want to leave a positive moral and spiritual legacy. Yet we know that in order to do that, we must be living out our moral and spiritual beliefs in the present. *Man Alive* shows how to make this desire a reality. I highly recommend this book to men of all ages."

> —GARY CHAPMAN, author of *The Five Love Languages*

"Something is missing from the average Christian man's life, but what is it? *Man Alive* gives men permission to dig down and discover the fire within."

> —CRAIG GROESCHEL, senior pastor of LifeChurch.tv and
> author of *Dare to Dr_____ ____ _____* and *Weird*

"No one understands what fi_____ at Morley. *Man Alive* is a page t_____ nk

about yourself and show you how to experience greater fulfillment in life. I highly recommend *Man Alive* for your personal reading or small group."

—NORM MILLER, chairman of Interstate Batteries

"*Man Alive* reminds me how God has wired me as a man and assists me in the challenging goal of aggressively living my life as God intended."

—BRIAN DOYLE, founder of Iron Sharpens Iron

"A great many men I've met want so much to experience the rich and abundant life Jesus promised but don't. As a result, they feel dissatisfied, caught in conflicting emotions. Are you one? In *Man Alive,* Pat Morley—who has probably had more deeply personal conversations with men than anyone I know—goes straight to the heart of your dissatisfaction. He delivers a world of wisdom that will lead you to strength, confidence, and clarity."

—BOB BUFORD, founder of Leadership Network
and author of *Halftime* and *Finishing Well*

"Pat Morley has earned the right to be heard. And in this mustread book, his commitment to men has risen to even a higher level. If you are serious about experiencing God's best, then *Man Alive* is for you."

—DR. TONY EVANS, senior pastor of Oak Cliff Bible
Fellowship, president of The Urban Alternative,
and author of *Dry Bones Dancing* and other books

"Dr. Patrick Morley is arguably the world's expert on what makes men tick. His thirty years of research and ministry in thousands of churches has given him a rich perspective on what it takes to build a powerful disciple-making ministry to men. His new book, *Man Alive,* goes to the heart of what men urgently need today. I urge you to read it for yourself, then recommend it to another man you care about."

—LEARY GATES, president of the National Coalition
of Ministries to Men and founder of BoldPath
Life Strategies

"Patrick Morley knows men. I know. I'm his pastor. I've watched God use him to transform our community during his many years of faithfully discipling men. And now, he's written *Man Alive* to transform you. This book will answer your most personally compelling questions and help you overcome the roadblocks to the abundant life. I have personally benefited from his insightful application of Scripture. His writings help me be a more effective pastor. Pat Morley is a spiritual mentor for us all!"

—DR. JOEL C. HUNTER, senior pastor of Northland,
a Church Distributed in Longwood, Florida

"When we were little boys, we all had big dreams about making an impact and leaving the world a better place. Yet something happened to most of us on the way to manhood. Almost inexplicably, those dreams got squeezed out. How did that happen? And is there anything we can do about it? Well, I have good news!

Patrick Morley has demystified this hard-to-understand phenomenon and drafted a clear-cut plan for you to become the man God
created you to be—a man fully alive!"

—H. Wayne Huizenga Jr., president of Huizenga Holdings

"Pat has done it again. He hits directly where so many of us find
ourselves—needing a compelling but realistic game plan to align
our lives with God's intentions."

—Steve Reinemund, dean of business at Wake Forest
University and retired chairman and CEO of PepsiCo

MAN ALIVE

TRANSFORMING YOUR 7 PRIMAL NEEDS
INTO A POWERFUL SPIRITUAL LIFE

PATRICK MORLEY

BEST-SELLING AUTHOR OF
THE MAN IN THE MIRROR

MULTNOMAH
BOOKS

Man Alive
Published by Multnomah Books
12265 Oracle Boulevard, Suite 200
Colorado Springs, Colorado 80921

All Scripture quotations, unless otherwise indicated, are taken from the Holy Bible, New Living Translation, copyright © 1996, 2004, 2007. Used by permission of Tyndale House Publishers Inc., Carol Stream, Illinois 60188. All rights reserved. Scripture quotations marked (NIV) are taken from the Holy Bible, New International Version®, NIV®. Copyright © 1973, 1978, 1984 by Biblica Inc.™ Used by permission of Zondervan. All rights reserved worldwide. www.zondervan.com.

Details in some anecdotes and stories have been changed to protect the identities of the persons involved.

A few concepts in *Man Alive* have appeared in various stages of development in earlier books, especially *Pastoring Men,* copyright © 2008, published by Moody, and *The Man in the Mirror,* copyright © 2000, published by Zondervan.

ISBN 978-1-60142-386-3
ISBN 978-1-60142-387-0 (electronic)

Cover design by Kevin McMillan

Published in association with the literary agency of Wolgemuth & Associates Inc.

Published in the United States by WaterBrook Multnomah, an imprint of the Crown Publishing Group, a division of Random House Inc., New York.

Multnomah and its mountain colophon are registered trademarks of Random House Inc.

Library of Congress Cataloging-in-Publication Data
Morley, Patrick M.
  Man alive : transforming your seven primal needs into a powerful spiritual life / Patrick Morley. — 1st ed.
      p. cm.
  ISBN 978-1-60142-386-3 (alk. paper) — ISBN 978-1-60142-387-0 (electronic)
  1. Christian men—Religious life. I. Title.
  BV4528.2.M668 2012
  248.8'42—dc23

                              2011044864

Printed in the United States of America
2012

10 9 8 7 6 5 4 3 2

Special Sales
Most WaterBrook Multnomah books are available at special quantity discounts when purchased in bulk by corporations, organizations, and special-interest groups. Custom imprinting or excerpting can also be done to fit special needs. For information, please e-mail SpecialMarkets@WaterBrookMultnomah.com or call 1-800-603-7051.

To Ed Cole, Hal Wilson, and Randy Chrastina,
my father-in-law and two brothers-in-law,
each uniquely a "man alive."

CONTENTS

1

POWERFUL, TRANSFORMED YOU

As stories began to emerge after the collapse of the World Trade Center towers, several survivors from the South Tower mentioned a courageous young man who mysteriously appeared from the smoke and led them to safety. They did not know who this man was who saved their lives, but this they remembered: wrapped over his mouth and nose was a red bandana.

For fifty-six minutes the man in the red bandana shouted orders and led people down a stairwell to safety. "I found the stairs. Follow me," he would say. He carried one woman down seventeen flights of stairs on his back. He set her down and urged others to help her and keep moving down. Then he headed back up.

A badly injured woman was sitting on a radiator, waiting for help, when the man with the red bandana over his face came running across the room. "Follow me," he told her. "I know the way out. I will lead you to safety." He guided her and another group through the mayhem to the stairwell, got them started down toward freedom, and then disappeared back up into the smoke.

He was never seen again.

Six months later, on March 19, 2002, the body of the man with the red bandana was found intact alongside firefighters in a makeshift command center in the South Tower lobby, buried under 110 stories of rubble.

Slowly the story began to come out. His name was Welles Crowther. In high school he was the kid who would feed the puck to the hockey team's worst player, hoping to give his teammate that first goal. He became a junior volunteer firefighter in Upper Nyack, New York, following in his dad's footsteps.

■ ■ ■

He was willing to go up while everyone else was coming down.

■ ■ ■

Welles graduated from Boston College, where he played lacrosse, always with his trademark red bandana. His father had always carried a blue bandana.

After college he worked as an equities trader on the 104th floor of the South Tower. He had a habit of putting change in his pocket in the morning to give to street people on his way to work.

Not long before September 11, Welles told his father, "I don't know how much longer I can keep doing this work." He was restless for more. Crunching numbers for invisible clients just didn't seem like what he was born to do. He dreamed of becoming a firefighter or public servant.

On September 11, 2001, at the age of twenty-four, Welles Crowther became both. And also a hero, because he was willing to go up while everyone else was coming down.

THERE MUST BE MORE

This story touches a need deep inside me—something so primal that I find it hard to put into words. But it makes me yearn to feel more alive. And every man with whom I've ever shared it has felt the same way.

Like Welles, we all want to make a contribution and leave the world a better place. It is a primal need—one among many. By "primal," I mean that as men we have a raw, restless energy that's different from women. It needs to be channeled, chiseled, transformed.

Over the last four decades, I've met one-on-one with thousands of men over coffee, in restaurants, in offices, online, after Bible studies, or just hanging out at the racetrack—men like you. I've listened to their stories. I've heard what they said and didn't say. Christian men know—or strongly sense—that we were created to lead powerful lives transformed by Christ.

But something is blocking them.

■ ■ ■

As men, we have a raw, restless energy that's different from women. It needs to be channeled, chiseled, transformed.

■ ■ ■

With a few inspiring exceptions, most men I talk to are confused about what a powerful, transformed life really looks like, regardless of how much "I love Jesus" they've got. They have high hopes for what Christianity offers but little to show for it.

Their instincts are screaming, *There must be more!*

When men try to put into words what keeps them from feeling fully alive, they invariably describe one or more of these seven symptoms:

- ■ "I just feel like I am in this thing all alone."
- ■ "I don't feel like God cares about me *personally*— not really."
- ■ "I don't feel like my life has a purpose. It seems random."
- ■ "I have a lot of destructive behaviors that keep dragging me down."
- ■ "My soul feels dry."
- ■ "My most important relationships are not working."

▪ "I don't feel like I'm doing anything that will make a difference and leave the world a better place."

Do you feel the angst? Do you see yourself on this list? As you can see, as men, our similarities dwarf our differences.

These inner aches and pains—these yearnings—correspond to the seven primal, instinctive needs we'll be exploring in this book.

THE HIGH COST OF BEING HALF ALIVE

I'd estimate that as many as 90 percent of Christian men lead lukewarm, stagnant, often defeated lives. They're mired in spiritual mediocrity—and they hate it.

Despite their good intentions, after they "walk the aisle" and "pray the sinner's prayer," most men return to their seats and resume their former lives. They don't take the next steps. Almost imperceptibly, one disappointment at a time, the world sucks out their newfound joy and passion for life in Christ.

▪ ▪ ▪

Almost imperceptibly, one disappointment at a time, the world sucks out their new-found joy and passion for life in Christ.

▪ ▪ ▪

Men lose heart, go silent, and anesthetize their pain. Then

they give up, burn out, drop out, or just slowly drift away. It's not just getting older; it's an assassination of the soul.

And isn't that exactly what the enemy of our souls wants? As Jesus said, referring to the devil, "The thief's purpose is to steal and kill and destroy" (John 10:10).

No man fails on purpose. None of us wakes up in the morning and thinks, *I wonder what I can do today to irritate my wife, neglect my kids, work too much, and have a moral failure.* But many of us will.

The statistics are jarring:

- 80 percent of men are so emotionally impaired that not only are they unable to *express* their feelings, but they are even unable to *identify* their feelings.
- 55 percent of marriages experience financial dishonesty, and it's usually the husband.
- 50 percent of men who attend church actively seek out pornography.
- 40 percent of men get divorced, affecting one million children each year.

The collateral damage is staggering. Tonight, one-third of America's seventy-two million children will go to bed in a home without their biological dad. But perhaps the greatest cost to the *physical* absence of fathers is the *practical* absence of mothers. Essentially, one person must now do the work of two. As a young woman who grew up without a dad said, "When my mom and dad divorced, I didn't just lose my dad. I also lost my mom, because she had to work long hours to support us."

A man leaves. A woman weeps herself to sleep. A little girl prays, "God, why is my daddy always so angry with me?" The men problem has made Dr. Phil a very rich man.

There has to be a better way.

WHAT A MAN ALIVE DOES DIFFERENTLY

We all know a handful of Christian men we admire more than others. Their faith has become robust and powerful. They're living lives of influence because their primal needs have been fulfilled. They feel alive. Perhaps you have even witnessed their transformation from spiritual mediocrity. Likewise, you've known men who never seem to be able to get it together spiritually. What makes the difference?

To ask, What do men who lead powerful, transformed lives do? would be misleading. Why? Because lukewarm men are just as likely to do a lot of those same things: attend church, serve on a committee, and send kids to youth group.

The right question to ask is, What do men who lead powerful, transformed lives do *differently* than their lukewarm counterparts? In business we call these the differentiated success factors.

To imitate what *most* professing Christian men do wouldn't be helpful. What we want to know is, What are the guys who really have it together doing that the guys who live in spiritual mediocrity don't do? What differentiates strong men from those guys who always seem to be looking in from the outside? What do successful Christian men do that unsuccessful Christian men fail to do?

■ ■ ■

The right question to ask is, What do men who lead powerful, transformed lives do *differently* than their lukewarm counterparts?

■ ■ ■

WHAT'S GOING ON?

Jesus gave us a picture of both the problem and the solution in His well-known parable of the four soils. A sower went out and scattered the seed of God's Word on four kinds of soil: the hard path, the rocky soil, the thorny ground, and the good soil.

Most men today would recognize themselves in the first three soils, where the seeds don't grow. Yet they honestly want to be like the good soil where the fourth seed fell—to be men "who truly hear and understand God's word and produce a harvest of thirty, sixty, or even a hundred times as much as had been planted" (Matthew 13:23).

What is keeping men's lives hard, rocky, and choked with thorns when so many urgently want more and when God created us for more—much more?

And, positively, what do men who lead powerful, "a hundred times" lives do differently than their mediocre counterparts? Jesus gave us an insight when He was speaking to a group of confused religious men. He said,

> Your mistake is that you don't know the Scriptures, and you don't know the power of God. (Matthew 22:29)

Do you see it? Jesus made a direct connection between knowing the Bible and leading a powerful life. Lukewarm men are in error because they "don't know the Scriptures" and therefore "don't know the power of God." Their *capabilities* don't equal their *intentions*. Without the right training, their soil remains bare, stony, and full of weeds. And as you'll soon see,

▪ ▪ ▪

Digging into the Word of God is easily the number one factor that differentiates men who have tapped into God's power.

▪ ▪ ▪

by "know the Scriptures," Jesus was talking about a lot more than mere head knowledge.

On the other hand, transformed men "truly hear and understand God's word and produce a harvest." Digging into the Word of God is easily the number one factor that differentiates men who have tapped into God's power.

A POWERFUL LIFE

The word "power" in the Bible is the Greek word *dunamis,* from which we get *dynamite.*

An army chaplain had a huge boulder in his backyard that he wanted to get rid of. He knew an army explosives expert, so he asked for help. The chaplain suggested they put some dynamite on top of the rock to break it up.

The explosives expert laughed. He said, "If we just detonated explosives on top of the rock, it would barely take a chip out of the rock—and we would shatter every window within a two-block radius!

"But I can do anything with that rock you want. I can leave the rock intact and throw it anywhere in your backyard you want. If you want it split in two, I can do that. If you want me to pulverize it, I can make that happen. You just tell me what you want, and I can shape a charge that will direct the power of the blast to do whatever you want."

That's the kind of immense, versatile power that Jesus envisioned in making the statement in Matthew 22:29. He had the same thought in mind later when He said, "You will receive *power* when the Holy Spirit comes on you; and you will be my witnesses" (Acts 1:8, NIV, emphasis added).

In the Scriptures and in the Holy Spirit, you already have at your disposal the power—the dynamite—of God to change your life.

WHERE DO WE GO FROM HERE?

What I'm proposing in this book is a huge promise—not from me, but from God's Word. Jesus said it Himself:

My purpose is to give them a rich and satisfying life. (John 10:10)

That's quite a promise.

The premise of this book is that you don't have to settle for being half alive. You can heal each of your inner aches and pains. You can be the good soil. You can be transformed. God will change your life one verse at a time.

■ ■ ■

You don't have to settle for being half alive.

■ ■ ■

It's not self-indulgent for you to become the man God created you to be. In fact, it's your destiny to lead a powerful life transformed by Christ—not without ongoing opposition but equipped and trained with the power to prevail.

I'm going to show you how God has provided ways for you to transform that raw, restless energy you feel into a powerful spiritual life. In each of the following chapters we're going to flesh out one of these seven primal needs:

1. To feel like you don't have to do life alone
2. To believe—*really* believe—that God loves and cares about you personally
3. To understand how your life has a purpose, that your life is not random
4. To break free from the destructive behaviors that keep dragging you down
5. To satisfy your soul's thirst for transcendence, awe, and communion
6. To love and be loved without reservation
7. To make a contribution and leave the world a better place

We'll explore how it feels when your life is not going right, what makes it so hard, and what to do about it.

I'm praying that God will satisfy your hunger for a powerful, transformed life and will supernaturally elevate you to a whole new level of feeling alive, from which you refuse to return.

We are part of something bigger than ourselves, you and I. We share a common bond. And there are others too—millions of us. Everywhere. Men unwilling to settle for spiritual mediocrity. Men unwilling to settle for anything less than becoming fully alive.

Let's go get it.

■ ■ ■

We are men unwilling
to settle for
spiritual mediocrity.

■ ■ ■

REFLECTION AND DISCUSSION QUESTIONS

1 "As men we have a raw, restless energy that's different from women. It needs to be channeled, chiseled, transformed" (page 5). Do you agree or disagree? Explain your answer.

2 In your experience, what do men who lead powerful, transformed lives do differently than men who are stuck in spiritual mediocrity?

3 The promise of this book is that you can lead a powerful life transformed by Christ. You don't have to settle. Which of the seven symptoms (page 6) do you most identify with? What would you like to see change?

2

EVERY MAN HAS a STORY

THE PRIMAL NEED: TO FEEL LIKE I DON'T HAVE TO DO LIFE ALONE

One day I received a phone call from the FBI. The agent said he wanted to ask a few questions about a friend of mine who had applied for a job at Homeland Security.

"Sure, fire away," I said.

"No sir," he said. "I need to do this in person." He insisted on a face-to-face meeting.

The next day, as the agent sat across the desk from me, I noticed that he looked tense. After a few routine questions about the nature of my relationship with my friend, he asked, "Have you ever been in his home?"

"Yes, of course!" I said. As if on cue, he relaxed. His change in body language and expression was so noticeable that I remarked about it.

Here's what he told me. "Over the years I've interviewed a lot of personal references who claim to be good friends with the applicant. But what I usually find is that they barely know each other. They can't tell me even the most basic details about the person, like where he lives or how many children he has. But real friends have generally been in each other's homes. I use that as a litmus test."

Think for a moment about the men in your life who know you best—the ones you call your best friends. Have you been in each other's homes?

If you're a father, how many of your friends know the names of your children? Or even how many children you have? And to keep this real, do you know the names of your friends' children?

As a practical matter, most men live in isolation. That doesn't mean we're hermits. We talk to other men during the day. We have a lot of acquaintances and at least a man or two we consider friends. But our relationships tend to be shallow. If we're not talking about work issues, we usually stick to news, sports, and weather.

It's not hard to see how this happens. From our earliest days, all the caregivers who help us become men—parents, grandparents, teachers, coaches, pastors—teach us that we need to take responsibility for our lives. And that's good, because no one else is going to do your homework, provide for your family, or make your rent or mortgage payment. We are wired by God to be responsible—to lead, protect, and provide.

But few of us are prepared for the "ouch" factor that goes

along with becoming a man. Even the happiest childhood includes memories of being teased, bullied, betrayed, and left out. And then we grow up only to discover that the bullies and the other mean people grew up too.

Let's face it. The world will chew you up and spit you out. The put-downs, cut-downs, sarcasm, snarky remarks, critical spirits, disrespect, disloyalty, lies, insults, betrayals, and jokes at your expense are real. Women are not the only ones who have feelings.

> Few of us are prepared for the "ouch" factor that goes along with becoming a man.

We don't need to go through many of these painful experiences before we think, *It's just not worth it.* Then we shut down. We become islands. Sometimes we're strong islands, sometimes weak ones, but in either case we're emotionally isolated. It just seems easier to go it alone. We live, work, play, and even worship in communities of strangers.

When crunch time comes, most of us don't have anyone to talk to. At least not anyone deeply invested in our success as a person. We end up feeling like we have to fight our battles on our own.

Of course, the problem with doing life alone is simple. It gets lonely—not right away, but inevitably. And when it hits, it hurts. The problem is that we were never meant to go it alone. We could say...

> *One of a man's most deeply felt needs is to feel like he is not in this alone—that he doesn't have to tackle life without others who care. Yet because of a man's tendency toward isolation, most men don't have deep, authentic relationships. In one way or another, men tell me all the time, "I just feel like I'm in this thing alone."*

Can you relate?

In this chapter you're going to see how living in isolation blocks men from leading powerful spiritual lives. Going it alone seems safe, but as it turns out, it makes us sitting ducks.

There *is* a better way. It's just that your enemy, the devil, doesn't want you to know about it.

ON THE OTHER SIDE OF ISOLATION

We all know from the National Geographic Channel that lions don't attack the herd. They go for strays. Every predator knows the strategic value of isolating prey—and we have a predator on our trail. "Stay alert!" warns 1 Peter 5:8. "Watch out for your great enemy, the devil. He prowls around like a roaring lion, looking for someone to devour."

An isolated man is a vulnerable man. When your gut keeps telling you, "I feel like I'm doing life all alone," that's actually a signal from God—His grace—to alert you to the danger. It's your signal to stop straying and to move toward meaningful relationships. But most men ignore the warning sign until it's too late.

I met Bill a few days after his wife served him with divorce papers. He was a wreck. He told me a sad story. "This was never what I wanted. But I lived like it was. All I ever did

∎ ∎ ∎

Every predator knows the strategic value of isolating prey—and we have a predator on our trail.

∎ ∎ ∎

was work, work, work. I neglected her and my kids. I have no friends. I completely isolated myself from people, and now I'm paying for it."

Does Bill's story strike too close to home for you? As men, we have an enormous capacity to sacrifice what really matters in order to get what doesn't. And then the lion pounces.

It's a guy thing.

I've discovered that men don't become isolated because they're wired that way. Quite the opposite. The truth is that you and I are wired by God with an instinct to be in authentic relationships so we don't have to go it alone. We are created to live in caring communities. It's our adversary who keeps whispering in our ear, "That's a bad idea." Remember, he's a thief who wants to destroy.

The Bible has such a different message. It says, "We are in this struggle together" (Philippians 1:30). It encourages us to "share each other's burdens" (Galatians 6:2). As Hebrews 10:24–25 says,

> Let us think of ways to motivate one another to acts of love and good works. And let us not neglect our meeting together, as some people do, but encourage one another, especially now that the day of his return is drawing near.

You don't have to go it alone or pay the high cost of isolation. On the other side of isolation lies a powerful force for personal transformation. It's hiding in a couple of highly potent words...

Your story.

THE POWER OF SHARED STORIES

In 1986 I started teaching the Man in the Mirror Men's Bible Study in Orlando. The book *The Man in the Mirror* was born there. Today 5,000 men from all walks of life join us each week to study the Bible together—150 men in person and the others over the Internet. After the message, the men discuss a few questions in small groups that gather in conference rooms, restaurants, cubicles, and churches around the world.

One of my passions each week at our on-site Bible study is to lead the first-timers table after the message—those guys visiting the live group for the first time. Many attend because they're in a marriage, money, health, or work crisis, often of their own making. Many made a profession of faith at some point in their lives. But they tried to go it alone, and their lives have not turned out like they planned.

Without a place to share their stories and grow together in a community, these men haven't been getting much out of their faith. Most feel isolated and confused. Many are still Bible rookies, even decades after professing faith. You know the cliché: instead of having fifteen years of experience, they have one year of experience repeated fifteen times. Without the loving concern of a caring community, they haven't been accountable. They haven't been insiders who get to observe up close how other men *really* handle their life issues.

I explain to the first-timers that we typically see three kinds of visitors:

▪ The first we might call a seeker, or inquirer. He's a man who has not yet developed a personal faith in Jesus Christ but, for some reason, is starting to warm to the idea and wants to know more.

■ The second kind we might call a new Christian. This is a man who recently made a profession of faith in Christ and now wants to know more about the faith he signed up for.

■ Let's call the third kind a longtime Christian. Perhaps he was in a Bible study once but hasn't been in one for a while. Or maybe he's looking for a place to build some friendships with like-minded men. Or, as is often the case, he's a man who made a profession of faith five, ten, fifteen, or more years ago, but he's been living by his own ideas and his life has not turned out as he'd hoped. He realizes, or is beginning to realize, that he needs to get to, or get back to, a more biblical Christianity.

I know the transforming power of shared stories, so every week I ask each man to answer a simple question: "Where are you today on your spiritual journey?"

Guess what I've discovered. Since 1986, I cannot remember a single man who didn't want to share his story.

Many of these men have never shared their personal stories out loud in a group before. These are men like you and me—men who have had others try to "fix" them, control them, betray their confidences, judge them, or hurt their feelings. So why share now?

The first thing we do at our Bible study is create a safe place for men to be real. I always say, "I know there are places you can go and give the wrong answer to where you are on your spiritual journey, because I've done that. But not here. Seriously, you could be on top of the mountain right now, or you could be down in a valley. Or you could be down in a valley under a pile of rocks. It just is what it is."

For many, it's their first exposure to a group of men talking honestly about their lives with transparency and vulnerability.

Second, our group is built around the Word of God. That means that each of the men just heard a

■ ■ ■

For many, the Bible study is their first exposure to a group of men talking honestly about their lives with transparency and vulnerability.

■ ■ ■

message in which I held up God's Word in front of them like a mirror. I lead them through some verses, explain what they mean, and show how they apply to everyday life. And because God's Word is so powerful, I know there's a good chance God has been speaking to them—even if they don't know it!

For the word of God is alive and powerful. It is sharper than the sharpest two-edged sword, cutting between soul and spirit, between joint and marrow. It exposes our innermost thoughts and desires. (Hebrews 4:12)

We've found that men who never thought they would enjoy talking in a group, men who have never shared personal

■ ■ ■

Because God's
Word is so powerful,
I know there's a
good chance God
has been speaking
to them—even if
they don't know it!

■ ■ ■

information with anyone before, and men who consider themselves loners all have this in common: once they start sharing their stories in a non-threatening environment, they no longer feel quite so alone.

It's that feeling of acceptance that keeps men coming back for more, even if they had always assumed they weren't joiners, talkers, or sharers. They feel valued and respected. And unlike men who don't have such a group, they get to experience the transforming power of a caring community.

Let me show you what I mean.

THE POWER OF A CARING COMMUNITY

My friends David and Ruthie Delk can attest to the power of belonging—or not belonging—to a caring community. Over the span of a year, they saw the marriages of four couples in their church start to fall apart. In each case the man had been unfaithful to his wife—a combination of adultery, pornography, solicitation of prostitutes, and going to strip clubs.

From a human perspective, there didn't seem to be any hope. Two of the marriages did fail, ending in ugly divorces and custody battles for teenagers. But the other two marriages have been restored.

What was the difference? The two failed men were on the fringe of their churches and not connected in relationships. That made it easier for them to walk away from their families. But the two restored men were being discipled by other men in small groups—men who wouldn't let them walk away from their families.

For example, one man with a pornography problem told his small group that he couldn't take it anymore and was going to bail. They said, "No, you're not. You're not going anywhere." Then they proceeded to affirm their love for him and express their sense of responsibility to walk with him through a restoration process. A few days later they showed up on his doorstep, seized his computer, cleaned off the porn, and installed filtering software.

The two restored couples are now helping others build and rebuild their marriages. Imagine how happy those wives are today that their husbands were connected to other men in a small group.

As someone said, "Never doubt the power of a small group

of committed people to change the world. That's about the only way it has ever happened in the past."

Here's another example. One day my younger brother, Pete, said, "My favorite day of the week was Tuesday. That's the day the new movie rental releases come out. My life had been so aimless that I was organizing my life around my favorite television shows and the new movie releases."

As a Christian, Pete didn't want to live like that. He had not been "running a good race." He was filled with self-loathing. But he felt powerless to do anything about it. Ten years earlier he had professed faith in Jesus, but not much had changed since. He had no one to help him. In fact, he rejected help. The first decade of his spiritual life was a spiritual roller-coaster ride. But recently Pete has changed. God has been knocking off the sharp edges. And he is starting to produce some spiritual fruit.

■ ■ ■

Imagine how happy those wives are today that their husbands were connected to other men in a small group.

■ ■ ■

I asked my brother, "What's going on with you?"

That's when he told me about Tuesday formerly being his favorite day. He explained that he had never read the Bible until a few years ago. That's when he was invited to be part of a weekly men's Bible study.

As he plunged into God's Word under the guidance of his leader and a group that accepted him, a transformation—a metamorphosis—started. It didn't happen overnight. After all, he had copied the behavior and customs of the world for a long time. But slowly the old Pete was dying. A different Pete was emerging—a truly different man, not merely a better version of the old Pete.

I love my brother so much. He insisted I use his real name and identity because he hopes you will be encouraged that if God can transform someone as off course as he was, he can transform you too.

Let's talk about how transformation happens.

IT STARTS WITH THE HEART

The word "transformed" in the New Testament is the Greek word *metamorphoo,* from which we get *metamorphosis.* It's what God envisioned when Paul wrote,

> Don't copy the behavior and customs of this world, but let God transform you into a new person by changing the way you think. Then you will learn to know God's will for you, which is good and pleasing and perfect. (Romans 12:2)

Christianity is *heart transformation,* not *behavior modification.* The reason that 90 percent of men lead lukewarm, often defeated lives is really quite simple. They're trying to solve the wrong problem. Most of us have the idea that Christianity is about behavior modification—using determination to change our behavior and be more spiritual. We think that if we can just get the right information, if we can just have more willpower and "man up," then we will do the right things and everything will be okay.

But everything is not okay. In fact, the harder we try, the more frustrated and confused we become. A man can only will himself to act and perform like a Christian for so long. One man who abandoned his faith said, "I served in the church for twenty years and I got worn out. I decided to try something else." Determination, we all learn eventually, is not a strategy.

How does heart transformation happen in practice? If we were to ask Pete, what would he say? He would tell us that his heart was transformed when he stopped trying to go it alone and dug into God's Word with a group of guys who accepted him "as is." He would tell us that he didn't really *do* anything. He simply presented himself to God as a flawed vessel, looking intently into God's Word in the company of a few men who cared about each other, and God changed the way he thinks.

That really is the story of transformation. It happens from

the inside out as we build our faith with each other. Everything starts with the heart. Jesus put it this way:

> The good man brings good things out of the good stored up in his heart, and the evil man brings evil things out of the evil stored up in his heart. For out of the overflow of his heart his mouth speaks. (Luke 6:45, NIV)

Authentic faith really is about the heart. Of course, Christianity is also about behavior, but it's behavior that overflows from changing what we believe in our hearts. Belief determines behavior. You could think of it like this:

right reading → right thinking →right believing → right behaving

In four decades of working with and serving men, I can't think of a single man who has ever consistently gotten transformation right without being part of a caring community focused on becoming disciples through the Word of God. Participation in a small group, or one-on-one, is a key difference between men who are spiritually alive and men who are mired in spiritual mediocrity. Turn the page to read about key criteria for building a thriving small group.

WHAT TO LOOK FOR
IN A SMALL GROUP

Jesus changed the world by inviting twelve men to join a small group. That was His strategy—to invest in men who would invest in other men. Simple. Powerful. Effective. Jesus understood that most meaningful change takes place in the context of small-group relationships.

If you want to change your life, you need to be in a small group for fellowship, Bible study, prayer, and accountability. One-on-one relationships with a skilled leader are also effective.

Why do some groups thrive while others languish or fail? My experience with small groups leads me to a short list of criteria:

- *The leader.* Everything boils down to leadership. There are all kinds of groups, but groups that change men's lives have a focused leader who is intent on making disciples.
- *A vision to make disciples.* The number one factor that distinguishes successful groups from those that accomplish little or nothing is a focus on discipleship and spiritual transformation.

■ *Love.* Men will come if they sense that the group really cares about them personally. Men have a nose for this. If it's not there, they will bolt—but rarely tell you why.

■ *Real conversation.* Any small-group format will work, including a one-on-one discipling relationship or a couple's home group, as long as the guys regularly have some private time to get real with each other. The best bet, though, is to join a men-only Bible study.

■ *Value.* Jesus offered men something they could find no other way—a changed life. Every time a man shows up for a small group, he has decided *not* to do something else. Most men have many choices, so your small group has to offer real value, or it won't last. So what do men find valuable? Every day men must venture out into a hostile world that beats them up and sends them home exhausted. A small group that gives men an opportunity to process why life is so hard and to ask real questions, such as, *Does God really care what happens to me?* or, *Does*

(continued on the next page)

He even know what's happening to me? is something real that men will line up for.

You'll know you've found a group that delivers value when you hear yourself saying or thinking things like:

- ■ "I really feel like my group cares about me personally."
- ■ "The leader makes sure I get a chance to air my thoughts."
- ■ "I cannot believe how my life is changing."
- ■ "I don't feel like I have to do this alone."

If you want to start a group, read the article "How to Lead a Weekly Men's Small Group" at ManAliveBook .com.

YOU ARE NOT ALONE

Now I want to ask you the same question I ask our first-timers: Where are you today on your spiritual journey?

Take a few minutes and give that question some serious, quiet reflection. I think you'll be surprised by what you learn about yourself. Be sure to take notes—those will come in handy later.

Unless it's just impossible, get with a few men once a week for an hour or two to discuss the questions at the end of each chapter. Share your stories with each other out loud—like we do at the first-timers' table. If you are not already in a group, it's easy to start one. You'll find a helpful discussion leaders guide at the end of this book. If it's a new group, consider calling yourselves the Man Alive Group.

■ ■ ■

No man wants to feel like he is doing life alone.

■ ■ ■

In this chapter we've seen that no man wants to feel like he is doing life alone, yet most do, sometimes with devastating results. God has provided a powerful way to solve this problem by giving us places where we can share our stories and grow together and where we can experience the transforming power of the Holy Spirit and the Word.

Are you ready to become part of a caring community of men? Or, are you ready to affirm your decision to be fully engaged in your existing group?

You don't have to go it alone.

REFLECTION AND DISCUSSION QUESTIONS

1 What is your litmus test for a real friend?

2 How has this group helped you pursue spiritual transformation and a powerful life?

3 Do we as a group feel that we are a caring community, that "we are in this struggle together" (page 24)? What, if anything, could we do better?

Answer this additional question if you are a new group:

4 In five to ten minutes, describe where you are today on your spiritual journey. (If your group needs more time for everyone to respond, you can meet longer for the first meeting or cover this question over more than one week. Don't rush this part.)

3

A Father in Relentless Pursuit

THE PRIMAL NEED: TO BELIEVE—REALLY
BELIEVE—THAT GOD KNOWS, LOVES,
AND CARES ABOUT ME PERSONALLY

During the summer after tenth grade, I had a terrible argument with my father and ran away from home. I rented an upstairs room in a house near downtown Orlando that had been converted into several rental units, three of which were upstairs. Those three rooms shared a single bathroom, a common sink, and a stove in the hall.

I found a job scraping dried cement off metal scaffolds, then dipping the frames in a tub of chrome-colored paint to prepare them for rental. I worked outdoors under a scorching sun that bounced all those ultraviolet rays off the chrome paint. Even my eyeballs got sunburned!

The next two weeks were an adventure. I ate grilled cheese sandwiches for dinner every night at the bowling alley across the street. I hitchhiked wherever I went. Frankly, I'm not sure what I had in mind—I certainly didn't have a plan.

By the end of two weeks, though, I was getting bored and

restless. That Friday night a friend came over and brought two six-packs of beer. We proceeded to drink our way through them, and then he threw up on my rug.

The next morning, head throbbing, beer cans strewn all over, I ached to go home. But I didn't know what to do. As far as I was concerned, I had severed all ties. I figured, once you left home, that was it—you could never go back.

Later that same morning I heard a knock on the door. When I opened it, there was my dad. I still have no idea how he found me. Hesitantly I invited him in. He stepped inside, looked around at the mess, and didn't appear to judge a thing. Then he looked at me. "Son," he said, "your mother and I just wanted you to know how much we love you. We were wondering if you'd be willing to come back home."

■ ■ ■

When I boil everything down, I can see that all I ever really wanted was to believe—really believe—that God loves and cares about me.

■ ■ ■

Well, he had barely finished speaking before I had everything I owned in a paper bag and we were out of there. All my grievances with him had melted away.

Today, I realize that I ran away because I didn't think my dad really cared about me. So I had started acting out. I was hanging out with the wrong crowd, doing all the wrong-crowd things. My dad tried to help, but we fought.

Of course, now that I've been a parent, I realize that when a father really loves his son, he must sometimes withhold what his son wants or make him do some things he doesn't want to do.

Here's why I'm telling you my story: because I had such a hard time believing that my dad really cared about me, it deeply affected how I thought about God. I've spent most of my adult life trying to accept the idea that my heavenly Father cares about me. When I boil everything down, I can see that all I ever really wanted was to believe—really believe—that God loves and cares about me. Not just in some theological sense either, but deeply and personally.

God loves Patrick Morley.

Pat, I love you.

By God's grace, I do know that now. But I must confess that it has taken decades. And, to be completely honest, every once in a while I still wonder, *Why would He care about me?*

Through my work I've discovered that we're all asking the same question: *Does God really care about me?* Unfortunately, except for the most spiritually mature among us, most men aren't so sure.

That's what I want to talk about in this chapter.

A MAN'S MOST TROUBLING DOUBT

You and I were created by God to be His sons, but it's natural for us to have doubts. Sometimes those doubts are big enough to make us run away. Yet we want to believe—really believe—that God knows, loves, and cares about us. It's one of our deepest, lifelong needs. In fact, based on what countless men have told me, I'd state this deeply felt need in even stronger terms:

> *Men want and desperately need to feel like God's much-loved sons—that He knows what we're going through, that He loves us in spite of our sins, and that He cares—really cares—about us personally. Yet most men find it hard to trust God for these things.*

Would you agree? How do you feel about it?

One day recently I was telling my friend Cameron, "By God's grace, I am absolutely convinced that God loves me. But it's more than that. I feel that God actually *delights* in me, that I am *pleasing* to Him, that He genuinely *likes* me!"

Cameron looked at me like I was from Mars. He thought for a moment, then he said, "Well, I believe God loves me, but I could never believe that He likes me. Not after all I've done. Love me? Sure. Like me? Not a chance!"

Like Cameron, many men don't feel worthy of God's

genuine affection and personal concern. They feel, in the words of Sigmund Freud, "morally despicable." They know too much about themselves and not enough about God's grace.

Gender researcher Terrence Real, in his book *I Don't Want to Talk About It*, noted that, unlike women, men tend to deny that they don't feel worthy and to pretend that everything is okay. These men overcompensate with macho behavior and shallow conversation meant to keep others—including God—at a distance.

Some men have had such a poor experience with their human fathers that they're stymied about how to relate to a heavenly Father.

My friend Jerry's father both physically and sexually abused him. His father also abandoned Jerry for extended periods of time in order to drive a long-haul truck. Today, Jerry has fully received Christ into his life and helps others in many ways. Yet he still feels the doubt created by his earthly father. He said, "I live every day with the fear of feeling the way I felt before I had God in my heart."

> ▪ ▪ ▪
>
> These men over-compensate with macho behavior and shallow conversation meant to keep others—including God—at a distance.
>
> ▪ ▪ ▪

Whatever the cause, not fully embracing the idea that God

really cares about you personally is the spiritual equivalent of running away from home.

But it doesn't have to be that way, because God does care about you. The Bible says, "Give all your worries and cares to God, for he cares about you" (1 Peter 5:7).

And God is adamant that we get this message. That's why He has given us the Bible, and the book's plot is actually very simple. In fact, the plot would make a great subtitle: "Loving Father Relentlessly Pursues a Relationship with His Children."

Your heavenly Father will never desert you, never abuse you, never fail to forgive you, never hold back His grace, and never condition His love on your performance. He's determined. He is in relentless pursuit of you, and He will not be denied. As I hope you will discover in this chapter, to be a son who is relentlessly pursued like that can turn a man around in his tracks.

Just ask Daniel Cummings, the son of Dan Cummings.

A FATHER WHO JUST WON'T GIVE UP ON YOU

Dan Cummings owned a bait-and-tackle shop on Florida's Gulf Coast. Soon after his son Daniel, a good kid, graduated from high school, Daniel started acting strangely. One night he didn't come home. He had been arrested.

In just six weeks following graduation, the eighteen-year-old Daniel became addicted to cocaine, stole a rifle, and traded that rifle to a drug dealer. But the police closed in and arrested the young man. He pleaded guilty, but because a firearm had been involved in the crime and then had somehow gone missing, Florida law required a stiff penalty. The judge sentenced Dan's son to ten years without the possibility of parole.

Dan said, "It was like someone ripped out my heart and soul." Unable to accept his son's fate, over the next year Dan spent his life savings of fifty thousand dollars on lawyers to free his son, all to no avail.

Still, he just couldn't give up. One day he got it in his mind that if he could recover the rifle, the judge might show leniency. It was the logic of the heart, to be sure, not a sensible legal strategy. But he was desperate.

■ ■ ■

The determination of the father had saved his son.

■ ■ ■

The only way to find the rifle was to enter the underworld of drugs. So Dan risked his life by buying information and running from drug lords. After several months, he found his son's drug dealer and was able to buy back the rifle.

At his son's mitigation hearing, Dan turned in the rifle and pleaded with the judge to reconsider. He told the judge how much he loved his son. He described how he had risked his life.

The court stenographer kept dabbing his eyes with a tissue. Tears streamed down the face of the clerk. Even the judge got a little misty.

After the emotional testimony, rifle retrieved, the judge suspended the sentence of Daniel Cummings to time served. The determination of the father had saved his son.

Do you have a father like that? One thing is for certain: you have a Father in heaven like that.

I know it's true because the Bible tells a similar story.

DESPERATE YOUNG MAN
SETTLES FOR PLAN B

A young man squandered his inheritance on wild living and prostitutes. During a famine, he came to his senses and reasoned, *Even my father's hired hands have enough to eat. I know what I'll do. I will go back to my father and say to him...*

> Father, I have sinned against both heaven and you, and
> I am no longer worthy of being called your son. Please
> take me on as a hired servant. (Luke 15:18–19)

This was his Plan B. So in desperation he rehearsed his speech and started for home. Then something unexpected happened.

While he was still a long way off, his father saw him
coming. Filled with love and compassion, he ran to his
son, embraced him, and kissed him. (Luke 15:20)

Then the son started to tell his father the speech he had
prepared: "Father, I have sinned against both heaven and you"
and the rest of it.

But the father had his servants give his son fresh clothes
and prepare a welcome-home feast to celebrate his return. He
explained,

For this son of mine was dead and has now returned to
life. He was lost, but now he is found. (Luke 15:24)

I want you to notice something in this familiar parable
about the love of God our Father.

The Bible says that the father in the story was filled with
loving compassion, ran to his son, threw his arms around him,
and kissed him. But notice that this happened *before* the son
ever spoke. In other words, the father's love was not conditioned
on what the son said. Before the son ever spoke, the father lav-
ished his love on his son.

You see, the father didn't have a Plan B. What he did have
was another Plan A.

This story is so precious to me. It's proof that God's love for

His children is unconditional. No doubt the father's next move depended on what his son said. If the son had been huffy, the father would have had to take a different approach. But he wouldn't have stopped pursuing his son with love.

■ ■ ■

You see, the father didn't have a Plan B. What he did have was another Plan A.

■ ■ ■

Back when I was a foolish teenager and my father showed up at my hideaway apartment, if I had said to him, "Who needs you anyway?" he would have had to take a different course of action. But he wouldn't have stopped being a caring father.

When we say that God is a loving Father who relentlessly pursues His children, that's a far cry from a timid God saying, "It sure would be nice if you came home." It's more like, "Everything in Me longs to be in right relationship with you, and I will not be denied. I will make a right relationship happen no matter how much you rebel, no matter how much you draw away—even if I have to orchestrate a worldwide famine like in the parable of the lost son. And if you take too long in coming to Me, I will hunt for you because I love you. You cannot escape My love. You are the object of My undying affection."

But maybe you still can't take it in. Sure, you'd like to, but you just can't. You know what you've done, what you're like inside. Why *would* your heavenly Father still love you?

YOUR VALUE TO GOD

Let me ask you to stop reading for a moment and take out your wallet. Pull out the newest bill in the highest denomination you have. Look at it carefully. If it's new, it looks crisp, doesn't it?

Okay, now I want you to crumple up that bill into a little wad. Pound it with your fist if you like. I'll wait…

Now unwad the bill and smooth it out. It doesn't look so crisp anymore, does it? So do you still want it? Of course you do.

▪ ▪ ▪

God has done for love what He would do for no other reason.

▪ ▪ ▪

Next I want you to crumple the same bill up again, then stomp on it several times. If you do it on a dirty floor, that's even better. I'll wait again…

Did that feel good? Now smooth out the bill again. It's starting to look a little tattered, isn't it?

Do you still want it? Of course you do! Why is that? Because the condition of the bill doesn't alter its value. That's *exactly* the way God feels about you.

Nothing you can do will ever make you good enough for God to love you. He loves you because He made you and because His Son, Jesus, gave His life for you.

On the other hand, nothing you can do will ever make you

bad enough for God to give up on you, no matter how tattered you look to outsiders.

God has done for love what He would do for no other reason. The Bible doesn't exalt any one attribute of God above the others. However, no other attribute of God—not His holiness, His greatness, His omnipotence, or His you-name-it—is adequate to explain why God would come to save us. The Bible expresses God's ridiculously generous love in these ways:

> How great is the love the Father has lavished on us, that we should be called children of God! (1 John 3:1, NIV)

> This is real love—not that we loved God, but that he loved us and sent his Son as a sacrifice to take away our sins. (1 John 4:10)

> For we know how dearly God loves us, because he has given us the Holy Spirit to fill our hearts with his love. (Romans 5:5).

There is no love like your Father's love. Because you are His son, God really does love you and like you. He is pleased with you and actually delights in you. Take it into your heart. You've never been loved, not really, until you've been loved like this.

TRUSTING GOD

Let's say you're there. There's one more key question: Can you really ever fully trust God to take care of you? We've all prayed and asked God for help when we've really been desperate, and nothing happened—like a marriage that failed, a child who didn't get well, losing a job, or retirement savings that went up in smoke.

When something tragic happens, it can't help but raise questions.

A friend's father committed suicide and left a note that said, "Trust God. He will take care of you."

My friend said, "Why should I trust God to take care of me? He couldn't take care of my dad."

Or maybe your father abandoned you in a different way, and you find it hard to believe that God won't abandon you too.

Jon Sheptock was born without arms, and his right leg is six inches shorter than his left leg. When his mother saw him at the delivery, she refused to even touch him and abandoned him to the state.

> "Jon, I don't know why God made you like this, but I do know how He thinks about you."

At six months of age, Jon was adopted by a loving couple. When Jon started school, every day the other kids would tease him without mercy. They would bully, push down, undress, or spit on him. And every day Jon came home from school in tears.

One day he asked his mother, "Why did God make me like this?"

His mother said, "Jon, I don't know why God made you like this, but I do know how He thinks about you." With that, she pulled out her Bible and read these words from Psalm 139:13–16:

> You made all the delicate, inner parts of my body
> > and knit me together in my mother's womb.
> Thank you for making me so wonderfully complex!
> > Your workmanship is marvelous—how well I know it.
> You watched me as I was being formed in utter seclusion,
> > as I was woven together in the dark of the womb.
> You saw me before I was born.
> > Every day of my life was recorded in your book.
> Every moment was laid out
> > before a single day had passed.

With those words of Scripture, God transformed Jon Sheptock's outlook on life. The world thought his deformity was an accident of nature. God's Word explained that God had made Jon exactly the way God wanted to make him.

That might be a mystery too big for you to understand. But it transformed Jon's life. Oh, it didn't make his circumstances any less tough. But it did change how he understood his identity. He humbled himself and came to a complete trust in God.

Today, Jon is married and has three beautiful children. He earns a living for his family through music and speaking.

It's one thing to believe that God loves you as one among many. It's another thing altogether to trust that God knows what you're going through, that He cares, and that He has the power and desire to watch over you personally.

Do you have that kind of trust in God? Would you like to? You've probably already figured out that it will never happen just because you want it to. And you're right. The timeless truths revealed in this chapter will change your life, but you have to respond and receive what God offers personally.

COMING HOME

Whether you've been away for two weeks, two years, or ever since you can remember, your Father loves you very much and wants you to come home by putting your faith in Jesus.

Faith in Jesus and repentance from sin are the foundation of a powerful life transformed by God. Where does this kind of faith come from? "Faith comes from hearing the message, and the message is heard through the word of Christ" (Romans 10:17, NIV). And what is Christ's message? "As the Father has loved me, so have I loved you" (John 15:9, NIV). Pause for a moment and consider how much love that must be. It's hard to take in, isn't it?

God wants you to know that no matter what you've done, you can be forgiven because Jesus loves you and died for your sins. This is what the Bible calls the gospel, or good news: "God showed his great love for us by sending Christ to die for us while we were still sinners" (Romans 5:8). The penalty for all your past, present, and future sins has been paid for by the sacrificial death of Jesus.

> ■ ■ ■
>
> Faith in Jesus and repentance from sin are the foundation of a powerful life transformed by God.
>
> ■ ■ ■

God wants you alive. "But because of his great love for us, God, who is rich in mercy, made us alive with Christ even when we were dead in transgressions—it is by grace you have been saved" (Ephesians 2:4–5, NIV). And not just in this life, but forever: "The wages of sin is death, but the free gift of God is eternal life through Christ Jesus our Lord" (Romans 6:23).

At 2:00 a.m. Kennon was lying in bed, listening through a set of headphones to a sermon on faith by John Piper and wondering why he didn't feel closer to his wife. He said later in an e-mail to me,

> I was desperate to experience God—to experience faith, to feel an affection for Him. For the first time, *faith as a gift* clicked—and heart and mind understanding formed into one. I asked God to experience faith in my heart, not just in my head—and I began to feel the weight of sin like I never had before. My sin became personal between me and God for the first time—I realized I had nailed Him to the cross. It crushed me and I felt my insides turning inside out, with an ache for forgiveness and desire for God—and instantly forgiveness and faith came, and I experienced a treasuring in Christ like I never had before. I gave my life to Jesus, not like the other times, but in real surrender. My tears of desperation quickly turned into tears of joy and I began laughing—because it was so simple, yet so mysterious, and I knew I had nearly nothing to do with receiving this gift other than accepting my need and then Him.

Can you relate to the ache Kennon felt? Do you feel like God is drawing you to also give—*really* give—your life to Jesus? You don't need any special knowledge to put your faith in Christ. Bishop William Temple wisely said that conversion is to simply give as much of yourself as you can to as much of God as you can understand.

But there is a caution. Receiving Jesus, having your sins forgiven, and receiving the gift of eternal life *is* easy, but only if it's sincere. Consider what happened to Julio:

> I prayed the sinner's prayer probably ten times. At first
> because I thought I would get something in return—
> like money, good fortune, and friends. Later, I prayed
> the prayer because I wanted some of my "Christian"
> friends to just leave me alone. But I never left my sin,
> never believed in my heart, never made Jesus Lord—
> not even for a minute. Until one night after years of sex,
> drugs, alcohol, and general debauchery, God drove me
> to my knees, and I cried out, "Please help me God—
> I need you, I cannot live like this anymore."

That night, Julio humbled himself and experienced the relief of salvation like Kennon did. And he is a changed and growing Christian today.

Praying a "sinner's prayer" is not the same as believing in Jesus, but prayer is a great way to express yourself if you really and truly want Christ in your life. If you're ready, here's a prayer you can offer right now and receive everything that Jesus promised. Let me suggest that you say it out loud because of Romans

10:9: "If you confess with your mouth that Jesus is Lord and believe in your heart that God raised him from the dead, you will be saved."

> Lord Jesus, I need You. Thank You for wanting me to experience the Father's love and acceptance. Thank You that I am valuable just the way I am. Thank You for loving me so much that You sacrificed Your life for my sins. By faith, I receive You into my life as my Savior and Lord. Thank You for forgiving my sins, for which I am truly sorry. Thank You for the gift of eternal life. Thank You for making me alive in You. Let me find rest for my soul. Change me into the man You created me to be. Amen.

If you just accepted Jesus Christ into your life, congratulations and welcome to the fellowship of much-loved sons! Any man who is walking with Christ will tell you the same thing: it's the single greatest decision he's ever made. Let me encourage you to tell someone right away—maybe your spouse or girlfriend, your pastor, a Christian friend, or the men in your *Man Alive* small

■ ■ ■

Any man who is walking with Christ will tell you the same thing: it's the single greatest decision he's ever made.

■ ■ ■

group. The act of explaining what you've done out loud will help you further conceptualize the significance of the step you've taken, and the positive feedback will encourage you.

WHAT IF YOU ALREADY KNOW GOD?

What if you have previously made a profession of faith in Jesus yet find yourself away from God and wanting to come home? Maybe you strayed off course. Maybe you got caught up in some sinful behavior. Maybe you had a major setback. Maybe you've lost hope.

As we learned from the parable of the lost son, your heavenly Father is always waiting with open arms. There are many ways to leave the Father but only one way to come back home.

■ ■ ■

There are many ways to leave the Father but only one way to come back home.

■ ■ ■

Or what if you *are* walking with the Lord, you *do* love Him with all your heart, and you *have* fully surrendered to the lordship of Jesus—but you *still* struggle to trust and accept that God loves and likes you? If, for example, you've had a rocky relationship with your human father, this may be a lifelong struggle—I know it has been for me. But you can live by the truth of God and not your emotions.

Here's a prayer you can pray now or anytime you find yourself not walking rightly with God or whenever doubts creep in:

Lord Jesus, I need You in my life right now more than I ever have. I *want* to come home. I *need* to come home. You are my God. Yet I have struggled to believe—really believe—that You know about me and care about me personally and that I can trust You. I would like to settle this right now. I have done sinful things of which I am ashamed. I know that I will never be good enough to earn Your love. Instead, You love me because You made me. You know me full well. And by faith I accept in my heart that You care about me and that I can trust You. I do love You. Help me to love You more. Forgive my sins. I invite You to once again take Your place as the Lord of my life. Continue changing me into the man You created me to be. Amen.

If you just prayed this prayer of renewal, congratulations! Trusting that God loves and cares about you is foundational to leading a transformed life. In the chapters ahead, we're going to build on this foundation so you can release the full power and potential of God's love into every need of your life.

REFLECTION AND DISCUSSION
QUESTIONS

1 Which of the stories in this chapter did you most relate to and why—my dad and me, the prodigal son and his father, one of the friends I mentioned (such as Cameron, Jerry, or my friend who's dad committed suicide), the boy on drugs and his father, Jon Sheptock, Kennon, or Julio?

2 Have you been able to accept—to really believe and trust—that God loves you, that He takes delight in you, that you are pleasing to Him, and that He actually likes you? If not, what is holding you back?

3 Did you pray either of the two prayers in this chapter (pages 59 and 61), and if so, why?

4

CREATED FOR A
LIFE OF PURPOSE

THE PRIMAL NEED: TO BELIEVE
THAT MY LIFE HAS A PURPOSE—
THAT MY LIFE IS NOT RANDOM

A frustrated young man in his teens asks me, "What's the point? What is my life supposed to be all about?"

A man in his late sixties, with tears in his eyes, tells me, "I don't know what to do. I just don't feel like I have any reason to get out of bed in the morning."

Whether we're young or old, no unmet need troubles us more deeply than feeling like our lives have no purpose. It starts growling when we're young, and until it's satisfied in God's way, it will just keep chewing us up.

This frustration is even more acute for Christian men, not because we think that finding our purpose isn't possible, but because we're sure it is. That's what the Bible says, and that's what we've been taught.

That's certainly been my experience. I grew up a religiously curious kid, but no one in my church took me under his wing. So I floundered. By high school the suffocating pointlessness of my life got the better of me, and I quit school in the middle of my senior year to join the army.

From day one, the army gave me a reason to exist: to serve my country. Immediately, I started to thrive. I was even inspired to take the GED and attend night classes at the Fort Bragg extension of North Carolina State University. Within three years I had completed my freshman year of college.

Then came my discharge papers. Suddenly my purpose was gone, and I had to start over again. So I came up with a new reason for living: to make a lot of money. After completing college, I went into real estate because that was the most expensive thing to sell and that meant making the biggest commissions.

> ■ ■ ■
> I had a disease
> we might
> call success
> sickness.
> ■ ■ ■

My unspoken credo became "Money will solve my problems and success will make me happy." I would set a goal, work hard, meet the goal, and then experience euphoria. But two weeks later the good feeling was gone, and I would have to set a new goal. The new goal, of course, always had to be bigger, brighter, higher, faster, or more expensive than the one before.

But all those met goals became a string of hollow victories, increasingly unable to deliver the fulfillment I craved. I had a disease we might call success sickness. It's the disease of always

wanting more but never being happy when we get it. 1
erable. And angry.

I started taking my frustrations out on my wife, Patsy. One
morning I was ranting, trying to find words that might relieve
the pressure building up inside. She just sat there, taking it in,
but soon I noticed big tears streaming down her face. She asked,
"Pat, is there anything about
me that you like?"

That was as low as I've ever
been. Ashamed, I went to work,
stared out the window of my
fancy office, and asked myself,

> It began to dawn on
> me that there must
> be a higher purpose.

*What's happened to you? You have everything you ever wanted—a
beautiful wife, a wonderful home, a great career. And yet you're just
as miserable as you were the day you quit high school.*

It felt like what Solomon said when he had it all: "Everything was meaningless.... So I hated life" (Ecclesiastes 2:11, 17,
NIV). Can you relate?

I'd always known that I couldn't settle for random. I had a
deep and compelling need for my life to have a purpose. But the
purpose I had chosen betrayed me, and once again, I was
headed back to the drawing board.

It began to dawn on me that there must be a higher purpose—a North Star that would shine from outside my life and
lead me to where I was created to go.

There is.

And it doesn't matter where you are right now. Whether you're frustrated, confused, angry, sad, miserable, in despair, floundering, resigned, or just looking for clarity, you can get there from here. That's what we're going to talk about in this chapter.

FEELING THE NEED FOR A PURPOSE

Men tell me all the time that they feel like their lives lack purpose. You've probably said things like this to yourself:

- *Is this it?*
- *What's it all about?*
- *Where's this going?*
- *Why am I here?*
- *I feel like I'm missing it. I'm not even sure I know what 'it' is.*
- *There must be more. There's gotta be.*
- *I feel like a ship without a rudder.*

We could sum it up like this:

A man has an urgent need to feel that his life has a purpose, that his life is going somewhere, that he has a reason for living, and that his life is not random. Yet most men don't know God's purpose for their lives.

Terry came from a middle-class family and built up a million-dollar business. But at the age of thirty-five, he was burned out. He said, "Money was my god, and I pursued it hard. The problem was that I caught my god." He became so depressed that he sold his company and entered counseling, where he learned that his purpose had been too small.

Like a lot of men, Terry had been a churchgoer all his life but didn't know he wasn't a Christian. Once he understood God's love and grace, he eagerly embraced Jesus. In time, Terry went back into business—bigger than ever—but with a whole new purpose and reason to exist.

What is the whole new purpose of a Christian that Terry discovered?

GOD'S BIG HOLY AUDACIOUS GOAL

Researchers wanted to find out what made America's great companies different from their mediocre counterparts. They discovered that the most successful companies set shockingly bold goals that inspired fanatical loyalty from their employees.

For example, Google's goal is "to organize the world's information and make it universally accessible and useful." Walmart's goal was to become the world's largest retailer. To explain this phenomenon, *Built to Last* authors Jim Collins and Jerry Porras coined the term "Big Hairy Audacious Goal," or BHAG for short.

God has a BHAG for your life—a shockingly bold goal. In God's case, it's a Big *Holy* Audacious Goal. It's clear. It's compelling. It's inspiring. And it's supremely simple. Once you become a believer, God's BHAG is for you to become His *disciple*. That is the whole new, higher purpose of your life.

> ▪ ▪ ▪
>
> God has a Big Holy Audacious Goal for your life.
>
> ▪ ▪ ▪

Stay with me and I'll show you how the ordinary, often-misused word *disciple* holds the secret to your God-designed need for a life of purpose.

What Is a Disciple?

The word *disciple* comes from the Greek word *mathetes,* which means "pupil," or "learner." When used in conjunction with Jesus, it came to mean "an adherent to the person and teachings of Jesus."

To be a disciple of Jesus is the highest honor to which a man can aspire. When Jesus called Peter, James, John, and the others, He called them to become what? Disciples. When Jesus left earth, the marching orders He left behind are to do what? "Go and make disciples" (Matthew 28:19).

Discipleship includes both the moment of *salvation* and the lifelong process of *sanctification.*

Here's an easy-to-remember definition. A disciple is…

- ▪ *called* to live in Christ
- ▪ *equipped* to live like Christ
- ▪ *sent* to live for Christ

Jesus said, "I will show you what he is like who comes to me [called] and hears my words [equipped] and puts them into practice [sent]" (Luke 6:47, NIV).

Let's break this down. First, a disciple is *called* to profess faith in Jesus Christ and abide in Him. This begins with the evangelism piece, or salvation. Without eternal life, religion doesn't mean

▪ ▪ ▪

To be a disciple of Jesus is the highest honor to which a man can aspire.

▪ ▪ ▪

much. I know because I grew up in a "Christian" home that didn't know Christ. We didn't reject the good news, because we never heard it. Our church was focused on other things. The results have been devastating. To be *called* also includes deepening our relationship with Jesus.

Next, a disciple is *equipped* by a process of ongoing spiritual teaching, growth, and transformation. To not disciple (train and equip) people who profess Christ will almost always mean they become lukewarm in faith, worldly in behavior, and hypocritical in witness. Evangelism without discipleship is cruel.

Finally, a disciple is *sent* to live for Christ by becoming part of a community, loving others, bearing much fruit, and doing good deeds. We each want to give our lives to a worthy cause. Once you have been with Christ—experienced the joy of His grace, the warmth of His love, the cleansing of His forgiveness, and the indwelling of His Spirit—you inevitably come to a point where you can no longer be happy unless you are serving the Lord.

What I most like about this biblical description of becoming a disciple is that it's *actionable*. It doesn't get lost in glittering generalities.

What does a disciple look like in everyday life?

How Jim Became a Disciple

Not long after Jim and his wife moved to Orlando, his new neighbor invited him to attend the Man in the Mirror Men's Bible Study. For six months Jim never said a word—not one peep. He later recalled, "If my table leader had asked me to talk, I would've been out of there in a flash and never come back. Somehow he knew not to push me."

One day his table leader asked, "Who would like to close us in prayer today?"

Jim spoke up, "I don't have much experience, but I'd like to give it a try."

For decades Jim had closed himself off from other people. He had been hurt so badly by his parents that he said, "I had no friends. I was afraid that if I cared about someone, they would just end up hurting me. So I walled myself in."

As Jim prayed, God took hold of his heart and began to change him. Through many small spiritual experiences and "coincidences," Jim felt *called* to live in Christ and so fully gave himself to the Lord.

A few weeks later he came to me and asked, "Is there anything I can do to help around here?"

I said, "Well, I need someone to go around to the table leaders about five minutes before 8:00 a.m. and give them the 'cut' sign so they can start wrapping it up."

"I can do that," he said.

A few weeks later Jim asked, "Is there anything else I can do?"

> "I had no friends. I was afraid that if I cared about someone, they would just end up hurting me. So I walled myself in."

I said, "Well, the man who has been bringing the orange juice can't do that anymore. Would you like to pick up the orange juice?"

"I can do that," he said.

Jim continued to ask for more assignments, and he was faithful with every one of them. After about a year, I said, "Why don't you become the Bible study administrator? I'll be in charge of teaching and you can be in charge of everything else." He liked that idea and held that position for seventeen years.

We decided to train our men in how to share their personal faith stories and how to lead a person to receive Jesus as Lord and Savior. Jim ate it up. He aced the work sheet that showed him how to explain what his life was like before Jesus, how he came to put his faith in Jesus, and what his life has been like since. He learned how to read Cru's (formerly Campus Crusade for Christ) Four Spiritual Laws pamphlet to someone and how to lead him in a sinner's prayer.

Jim was being *equipped* to live like Christ. He had no idea that God would soon call upon him to put his new skills to use.

A few months later, Jim received a phone call that his estranged son was in a hospital and about to die from AIDS. Jim and his wife caught the next plane to Cincinnati.

When they arrived on the hospice ward of the hospital, they were shocked to see the gaunt, fragile silhouette of their prodigal son hooked up to a menacing array of IVs and medical devices. After they regained their composure, God emboldened Jim to tell his son, "Tim, I love you very much." But Tim wasn't interested—he would have none of it.

Every morning for the next ten days, Jim and his wife came to Tim's room. Every day, the first thing Jim did was say, "I love you, Tim. You're a good man." And then he kissed his son on the forehead. Every day, his son rejected his father's love. Jim and his wife prayed for their son, but Tim didn't participate. They told Tim how sorry they were for their part in the estrangement and how much they longed for reconciliation. After many days of resistance, the wall of hostility began to crumble. Finally, Tim confessed to his mother, "Mom, I'm so sorry. I never gave Dad a chance."

On the tenth day of their vigil, the doctors told Jim and his wife that the end was near. They then told their son that he was about to die. Jim said, "Tim, God loves you and wants to forgive your sins and bring you to live with Him in heaven. If you ask Him to forgive your sins and ask Jesus to be your Savior, you can be with God when you die. Would you like to do that?" After some discussion, Tim asked Jesus to forgive his sins and give him eternal life. That was on a Friday. He passed away on the Sunday. Tim crucified his sins on Friday, and three days later he was raised from the dead.

> ■ ■ ■
>
> Tim crucified his sins on Friday, and three days later he was raised from the dead.
>
> ■ ■ ■

Jim helped two other young men with AIDS on his son's floor also receive Jesus just before they died. God *sent* him to live for Christ among men facing not only physical but also spiritual death.

Jim said later, "Leading my son to Jesus is the greatest thing

I've ever done. I shudder to think of what might have happened if I hadn't moved to Orlando, gotten into a Bible study, found my faith, grown to be a good Christian, and learned how to share my faith. When I look back, it's so clear that God has a purpose for my life, even though it felt pretty random at the time. Discipleship has changed my life. Praise God!"

We all admire a Welles Crowther who makes headlines for a single act of great courage. But let's also give a nod to the millions of men who, like Jim, are courageously living out God's plan and purpose each and every day in the details of their lives.

A PURPOSE, NOT A PANACEA

Jim's story also illustrates an important misunderstanding. A lot of men desperately hope that becoming a Christian will make their problems go away. But that's rarely the case. Jim's son still died.

Recently I polled the 150 or so men who attend the on-site sessions of the Man in the Mirror Bible Study:

- First, I asked, "How many of you are having work-related problems? If so, raise your hands." About 50 percent of the men raised their hands.
- Then I said, "Raise your hand if you or someone in your family is having a health problem?" Roughly 30 to 40 percent did so.

- ▪ Next I said, "If you're having money problems, please raise your hand." This time something like 60 percent raised their hands.
- ▪ Next I said, "If you are having some kind of a relationship problem, raise your hand." Again, about 50 percent raised them up.
- ▪ Then I said, "If you don't have any problems, raise your hand." A mere four men hoisted their arms.
- ▪ Finally I asked, "For those who just raised your hands indicating that you don't have any problems right now, how many of you lied?" One of the four men raised his hand, and we all had a good laugh!

It's important to your discipleship that you have a realistic expectation of how God operates. If you don't, you are sure to stumble. Being a disciple is a purpose, not a panacea. Becoming a disciple won't insulate you from problems. God doesn't eliminate the storms. Instead, like leading the Hebrews out of slavery in Egypt, storms are special opportunities for God to display His power in miracles. The Lord is just as likely to deliver you *in* a storm as *from* a storm.

So don't lose faith when troubles come, but believe that God will always take care of you one way or another. And rejoice that your problems—and how you handle them—will bring glory and honor to His name.

TAKING STOCK:
A DISCIPLESHIP POP QUIZ

One of the biggest mysteries of my career has been the large number of men I've met who believe that Jesus is their Savior but who have never really thought through what discipleship should look like in their everyday lives. That's why they say things like "What's the point?" and "I don't know what to do" about their lives.

How about you? Here's a simple three-question quiz to help you evaluate your own discipleship using the definition from earlier in the chapter: A disciple is *called* to live in Christ, *equipped* to live like Christ, and *sent* to live for Christ.

1. *Are you a man who has been called to live in Christ?* Have you truly and earnestly repented of your sins and placed your faith in Jesus alone by faith alone for the eternal salvation of your soul?
   ❏ Yes
   ❏ No

2. *Are you a man being equipped to live like Christ?* Equipping is about both doing private study and getting into caring

communities so that spiritual formation, growth, and transformation can take place. You have to be a participant, not a spectator, to be equipped. Are you involved in a process of becoming more like Christ?

❒ Definitely

❒ Mostly

❒ Somewhat

❒ No

3. *Are you living like a man sent to live for Christ?* A disciple is not just taking in. He is also giving out. He puts God's Word into practice. He sees and treats people like Jesus would. He is intentional about producing spiritual fruit through his family, his work, serving others, sharing the gospel, and other acts of ministry. Would a friend who knows you well conclude that you are a disciple on a mission to live for Christ?

❒ Definitely

❒ Mostly

❒ Somewhat

❒ No

So how did you come out? Don't worry if you don't feel like you're the apostle Paul yet. Remember, discipleship is a process.

What if you're new to discipleship or have misunderstood it? How can you get started?

GETTING STARTED IN DISCIPLESHIP

Brandon and his new wife both had been working long hours and were feeling exhausted. They decided to celebrate their first wedding anniversary with a romantic getaway weekend at an upscale North Carolina resort—just what the doctor ordered.

But instead of catching up on sleep and each other, they stayed busy taking in all the attractions. On Sunday they had a small lover's quarrel that unfortunately escalated throughout the afternoon.

By Sunday night, when they finally sat down to talk about it, she was in tears. After an hour of talking in circles, Brandon threw up his hands and said, "Look, right now you need to know that I don't feel anything—not for you, not for God, not for my work. I know I love you. I'm not going to leave. But I just feel numb."

The way he could deliver those words with such icy detachment scared Brandon. The next day he urgently called his pastor and said, "Kevin, I really need to meet with you right away.

I think my marriage is in real trouble, and I know that I'm in real trouble. Can I come see you?"

Kevin said, "Well, I'm pretty busy this week. How about next Tuesday?"

Brandon said emphatically, "No, you don't understand. I need to meet with you *right now*."

> ▪ ▪ ▪
>
> Brandon had never realized that *he* needed discipleship— that it was for *him*.
>
> ▪ ▪ ▪

When Brandon's pastor caught the gravity of the situation, he rearranged his schedule and they met. What his pastor discovered was a man who wanted to get it right. But even though Brandon was a believer and attended church, he had never realized that *he* needed discipleship—that it was for *him*. Or what it really was. Or how powerfully it could transform his life. As a result, he had never learned God's way to become a godly man, husband, and father. You don't know what you don't know.

After they handled the immediate crisis, Brandon realized that he needed to embrace his purpose of becoming a disciple. Kevin agreed to meet with him on a weekly basis to disciple him. In those one-on-one sessions, Brandon described situations in which he didn't know what to do, and Kevin related what the Scriptures have to say about it.

For his part, Brandon was eager. He really wanted to unlock the secrets of his faith and discipleship. It wasn't long until

Brandon started to feel alive at a level he had never experienced before.

That was two and a half years ago. Today his marriage is rock solid. Brandon and his wife now disciple other young couples and singles in their home during a weekly Bible study. God has radically transformed his life, and for the first time in his life, Brandon feels like he has something worth living for because finally he has something worth dying for. He found his North Star.

Have you realized that *you* need discipleship—that discipleship is for *you*?

Don't worry if you're not sure about how to become a disciple—that's what the rest of *Man Alive* is all about. One more thing...

GOD'S GUARANTEE

God has not left your purpose of becoming a disciple of Jesus to chance. God is not up in heaven wringing His hands about how your life will turn out. Instead, He's working out everything to conform to His will—the crux of which is His Big Holy Audacious Goal for you to become His disciple, to become like Jesus.

God's *everything* includes every relationship you have, every task you perform, every person you meet, every book you read, every sport in which you participate, every sermon you hear, every class you sit through, every small group you join, every mission trip you take, every radio program you listen to, every website you visit, every television program you watch, and every other thing.

Everything.

God doesn't do random.

Once you come to faith in Jesus, God guarantees that you will be transformed. He will not be denied. As the apostle Paul said,

> I am certain that God, who began the good work within you, will continue his work until it is finally finished on the day when Christ Jesus returns. (Philippians 1:6)

Ah, but there's a paradox. Because God also gives us the gift of free will, you can resist Him—actively or passively—and make the process much longer. So many men I know do just that. Frankly, it's heartbreaking to watch men numb themselves with substitutes. They don't just miss out on a soul-satisfying purpose; they end up feeling half alive. And not only are they miserable, but they suck the joy out of everyone around them too.

Friend, don't let this happen to you. Commit yourself to becoming a disciple.

In this chapter we dove into that urgent need we all have to feel like our lives are going somewhere and have a purpose—that life isn't random. God offers us a whole new and higher purpose—a North Star to lead us.

God's purpose, His BHAG, is for you to become His disciple. The Bible promises, even guarantees, that every genuine disciple will become like Jesus. It is the highest honor to which you can aspire—your true north.

REFLECTION AND DISCUSSION QUESTIONS

1 "No unmet need troubles us more deeply than feeling like our lives have no purpose.... This frustration is even more acute for Christian men, not because we think finding our purpose isn't possible, but because we're sure it is. That's what the Bible says, and that's what we've been taught" (page 65). Please comment.

2 What is a disciple?

3 Do you understand that God's purpose for your life is for you to become His disciple? What, if anything, has been holding you back from fulfilling it?

5

BREAKING THE CYCLE

THE PRIMAL NEED: TO BREAK FREE FROM THE DESTRUCTIVE BEHAVIORS THAT KEEP DRAGGING ME DOWN

One day my wife asked me what I was going to speak about at our Bible study the next morning. I said, "I'm going to be talking about repetitive sins."

She deadpanned, "So I guess you'll be speaking without notes."

Guys love it when I tell that story. (So do their wives.) Most of us understand what it means to be gripped by a pattern of destructive behaviors. We're either stuck in one now and we hate it, or we remember vividly what it was like and we can't believe how long it took to let go.

The apostle Paul described his own painful struggle in this area: "I do not understand what I do.... For what I do is not the good I want to do; no, the evil I do not want to do—this I keep on doing" (Romans 7:15, 19, NIV).

My friend Antonio told me, "I was five years into my second marriage before I realized that I didn't have a clue how to do intimacy or show my wife the respect she deserves. I hurt her so many times. But I was just doing relationships the way I'd seen them happen while growing up."

Fortunately, Antonio turned things around. The jury is still out on Brian though. Now almost fifty, Brian still can't tell you what he wants to do with his life. He rarely sticks with a job for long. You can imagine how this frustrates his wife and confuses his young adult sons.

Antwon's angry outbursts at coworkers have undermined his ability to get promoted.

> ■ ■ ■
>
> It's hard to believe we can break free.
>
> ■ ■ ■

Hector keeps telling lies at work and sabotaging his career.

William says he wants to change, but he keeps losing his battle to stay away from porn.

Many, if not most, men I know can point to negative, dumb, and harmful patterns of thinking and behaving that hold them hostage. We keep repeating the same destruction over and over. A friend of mine says, "Most of us are just one step away from stupid."

After fighting and losing the battle for a long time, it's hard not to think, *I guess that's just how I am.* It's hard to believe we can break free.

But we'd sure like to, wouldn't we?

Could life get that good?

That's what we're going to find out in this chapter—a chapter that, as you'll see, is close to my heart.

NOTES FROM A BROKEN BOY

In 1926, when my dad was two years old and the youngest of four children, his father abandoned the family. That one fateful decision set forces in motion from which our family has still not fully recovered.

My dad never felt the scratch of his father's whiskers, never tossed a ball in the backyard, never heard his father's voice reading him a bedtime story, never smelled his father's work clothes, never wrestled on the ground, never had his hair tousled, and never had a dad to mimic.

The driving force in my dad's life when he became a man was to not be like his father. Although I don't remember his ever using these words, he wanted to "break the cycle." My dad needed help. His heart was in the right place, but he had no example of manhood.

Help never came.

When the size of our family grew to four young boys, my dad had us join a church. But our church had no vision to help men like my dad become disciples of Jesus. As a result, none of the elders of the church saw this rookie husband and dad, knew what had to be done, and trained him up as a disciple. Instead, he was left to guess at how to be a husband to my mother and a father to my brothers and me. Mostly, he guessed right about how to be a good husband but wrong about how to be a dad.

For example, I have no childhood memory of feeling loved or hearing my parents say, "We're proud of you." I don't remember being comforted. I don't remember being held, hugged, encouraged, or told I was loved. As a result, I always felt like I was on my own.

■ ■ ■

None of the elders of the church saw this rookie husband and dad, knew what had to be done, and trained him up as a disciple.

■ ■ ■

My defense was to reject my parents. I decided that if they didn't need me, then I wouldn't need them either. When I was about ten years old, my parents said they were going to attend my Little League game. I begged them not to come until I was in tears, and finally they agreed to stay away. Then I threaded my glove onto the handlebars of my bike and cried all the way to the field because they were not coming.

Of course, I did want them to be there—badly. I wanted my parents at all my games. I wanted them to rescue me from what became a downward slide that ended with my quitting high school.

My next younger brother followed in my footsteps. He

eventually died of a heroin overdose. My other two brothers have had more than their fair share of struggles.

I grew into an adult who had a hard time believing anyone really cared about me. It's still a risky thing for me to accept someone's genuine love. Even then, to be honest, I never expect it to last.

I wonder if you can feel what I'm saying.

Thankfully, I didn't repeat the sins of my parents. But I did bring brokenness into my marriage and family. I was supersensitive, selfish, and easily angered. I had to start from scratch in learning how to trust Patsy when she said she loved me. And I had to learn how to love her back in ways that really spoke to her heart. On my side, it was marriage kindergarten for more years than I care to mention. But she stuck with me, and her faith changed my life.

And those repetitive sins? I'll share more in a minute, not just what happened but also how healing came for me and how it can for you too. For now, I'll tell you with real regret that I kept my family walking on eggshells for years.

It's hard to silence the echoes of the past.

THE GREAT ESCAPE

For the next few pages, I invite you to consider how men can break the cycle of generational brokenness. In my experience and in the experiences of most of the men I've talked to, these wounds often show up in our lives as impulsive, recurring sins.

Clearly, what happened to us or to those who raised us is not always the root of our present destructive behaviors. But the pattern shows itself often enough to be extremely troubling. That's why we need to give it a closer look in this chapter.

I would describe a man's deeply felt need in this area like this:

Men have a primal need to break free from the destructive behaviors that keep dragging them down. They are baffled that they can't break free. And it's embarrassing. They desperately want to experience freedom from their bondage to sin. They do their best to manage these behaviors, but what they really want is for the damage to stop. But they feel weak and stuck. Unfortunately, millions of us just don't know where to turn.

I know you know what I mean! Christian men have talked to me about the tyranny of behaviors they hate. They know that, in Christ, they are new creations. But day to day, they live like repeat offenders.

Meanwhile, they're passing brokenness down to the next generation—often just like it was passed down to them.

Why do these negative behaviors hold such a mysterious power over us? We all know the right theological answer: the world, the flesh, and the devil have us in a stranglehold. We might be able to point to a source—"I guess it's just in my genes" (nature) or "That's just the way it was growing up" (nurture). But as a practical matter, like the apostle Paul in the verse I quoted earlier, we're not exactly sure why we're slaves to sin.

I have good news.

That powerful desire to escape from persistent, habitual sins was placed in you by God. With His help, you can break free from the destructive behaviors that keep dragging you down. You can be healed. You can redeem the past. The damage to yourself and others can stop with you.

■ ■ ■

Meanwhile, they're passing brokenness down to the next generation—often just like it was passed down to them.

■ ■ ■

In this conversation about repetitive sins, stories are important. They show us that we're not alone and that we can break the cycle. That's why I want to share a little more of my story, along with the experiences of other men. And then I want to invite you to share your story.

My prayer is that by the end of this chapter you will

understand how intergenerational sin affects you, realize that you can close the book on your past, and believe—*really believe*—that God will empower you to make the great escape from bondage.

THE VOLCANO INSIDE

When my mother died, I experienced something odd: I didn't feel anything. That got me into counseling.

It didn't take long for my counselor to start coming to some conclusions. She said that I was a little boy with a hole. Something is missing, she told me, when we don't feel precious and deeply cared for. When parents don't touch their children, express affection verbally, and spend quality time with them, the children experience these shortcomings as a betrayal.

> Sure, I had wounds. But I had to decide if I was going to be a victim or a victor. We all do.

That really opened up a can of worms—and there were more worms in the can than I thought.

Over time I began to understand that I had been in denial about what had happened with my dad and mom. They had failed me. I also came to realize that what happened wasn't my fault. I knew my parents hadn't failed me on purpose—they loved me. But it happened anyway.

Once I finally accepted that the sins of the past genuinely affect the present, I could face and grieve the broken parts of my life. And I had a choice to make. Sure, I had wounds. But I had to decide if I was going to be a victim or a victor. We all do.

Christian author and counselor Larry Crabb said, "Biblical counseling must insist that the image of God is central to developing a solid view of personality; that our sinfulness, not how we've been sinned against, is our biggest problem; that forgiveness, not wholeness, is our greatest need; that repentance, not insight, is the dynamic in all real change."

I did face what I didn't get. I faced my own shortcomings too. I called sin, sin. I grieved. I forgave. I repented for all the boomerang sins I had committed against my parents and my wife and my children. The Holy Spirit cleansed me. Finally the healing of my past and the breaking of intergenerational sin began to seem possible.

But one step remained. I still needed to make amends for the repetitive sins. You see, the way I acted out my brokenness was through an angry spirit (a common way for men).

I remember the week I was preparing to teach on anger. I read,

> Do not be quickly provoked in your spirit,
>   for anger resides in the lap of fools.
>   (Ecclesiastes 7:9, NIV)

There's a huge difference between getting angry and having an angry spirit. To have an angry spirit is to be easily provoked to anger. If you have an angry spirit, it's like walking around with a volcano inside you, never knowing when it might erupt or why. That was me.

> ■ ■ ■
>
> If you have an angry spirit, it's like walking around with a volcano inside you.
>
> ■ ■ ■

I felt compelled to write a letter to my children. With their permission, I'll share part of what I wrote:

Over the last few weeks especially, God has brought to mind many, if not most, of the times I have exploded and lost my temper inappropriately with each of you. It has been painful, yet it has also changed my story about myself.

Frankly, it's embarrassing to confess this to you because all my life I wanted to be the perfect father, and now I realize that I was not. I ask you to please forgive me. I want to forgive myself, but I'm finding that hard, because I haven't brought this to you.

I love you very much and have always wanted and worked for your well-being. But now I realize that I must accept responsibility for having an angry spirit when you were growing up. I have already worked through this with your mother. Today, I am asking you to forgive me for the ways my angry spirit hurt you, and I am releasing you to God in prayer for whatever healing may be necessary in your heart.

Also, I realize you may have some things you want to say to me or ask me before offering me forgiveness. I would welcome the opportunity to hear from you about this. I will do anything for you.

I love you with all my heart,
Dad

Both of my children were gracious beyond words. I will always treasure their forgiveness and tender reassurances. And I can tell you that our relationships today are healthy and flourishing, and they are both strong disciples.

Own Your Stuff

Whatever your broken wing is, whatever keeps dragging you back down into a repeating pattern of sinful behavior, God can mend and transform those areas of your life.

Paul wrote in despair, "Oh, what a miserable person I am!

Who will free me from this life that is dominated by sin and death?" (Romans 7:24). Are you surprised that the great apostle Paul was so much like you and me?

Paul went on to answer his own question. He wrote, "Thank God! The answer is in Jesus Christ our Lord" (verse 25). Paul was like us, and his solution is our solution. The gospel of Jesus will deliver us, not only for salvation, but also for sanctification. That means we can apply the gospel of Jesus to the sins that keep dragging us down. This is one of the foundational ways we become disciples. Are you ready?

The starting point for cycle breaking is to own your stuff. No doubt the sins against you are real, perhaps tragic. But it's what you do next that counts. Will you take responsibility for yourself? Will you own the ways you have been repeating or extending the cycle? Will you humble yourself before your Creator and get out of denial? By all means, grieve what could have been. But then you need to take responsibility for what happens next, starting with godly sorrow. Paul put it like this:

> I am not sorry that I sent that severe letter to you,
> though I was sorry at first, for I know it was painful

to you for a little while. Now I am glad I sent it, not
because it hurt you, but because the pain caused you
to repent and change your ways. It was the kind of
sorrow God wants his people to have, so you were
not harmed by us in any way.... But worldly sorrow,
which lacks repentance, results in spiritual death.
(2 Corinthians 7:8–10)

Repentance is at the heart of the gospel. It's the foundation
of transformation and disciple making. *Repentance* literally
means "to change your mind." But repentance is not a once-for-
all step at the beginning of salvation. Martin Luther said it well
in the first of the Ninety-Five Theses he nailed to the door of
the Wittenberg church: "Our Lord and Master Jesus Christ,
when He said 'Repent,' intended that the whole life of believers
should be repentance."

Repentance is a commitment to see ourselves as we really
are, own it, and then allow the godly sorrow we feel to inspire
deep change. For example, I have hoped and prayed for this
book to be successful. I know I want success for the right reason—to help men understand and meet their primal needs.
But every few days my sinful nature will pop an idea into my
head—like enhancing my reputation or making big bucks.
Both of these motives can be good, but not when you want
them because of worldly ambition.

Whenever I become aware that my motives have gone rogue, even for something good, I stop, change my mind, and ask God to renew me. It works every time! But it doesn't make the sinful nature go away. Instead, repentance is like cutting a piece of string in half. No matter how many times you cut it in half, half is still left.

Repentance is not merely asking God to make us into better men; it's asking Him to make us different and to change our ways. Repentance is most effective as a lifestyle of daily, even moment-by-moment self-awareness. Why is it so important? It's hard to picture a man ever leading a genuinely powerful, transformed life apart from a lifestyle of repentance.

> ■ ■ ■
>
> Repentance is most effective as a lifestyle of daily, even moment-by-moment self-awareness.
>
> ■ ■ ■

So what if you're caught in a destructive cycle? No one can tell you to just get over it. If you were able to break the cycle on your own, you would have done so by now.

But God does not want you to be trapped in destructive cycles. In fact, He has put term limits on repeating the cycles. He has told us so in Scripture. When God appeared to Moses on Mount Sinai, He said,

Yahweh! The LORD!

The God of compassion and mercy!

I am slow to anger

and filled with unfailing love and faithfulness.

I lavish unfailing love to a thousand generations.

I forgive iniquity, rebellion, and sin.

But I do not excuse the guilty.

I lay the sins of the parents upon their children and

grandchildren;

the entire family is affected—

even children in the third and fourth generations.

(Exodus 34:6–7)

I want you to see how Moses responded, but before we do that, think for a moment about the greatness and goodness of God, His eternal power, His love, compassion, and forgiveness. Yes, sin affects entire family lines, but the text implies that God puts term limits on the destruction—a maximum of four generations. And that can be shortened by breaking the cycle now. But He lavishes His love on a *thousand* generations.

So what did Moses do when he heard about this wonderful grace?

Moses immediately threw himself to the ground and worshiped. (verse 8)

Now it's your turn. I'm going to show you how to throw yourself to the ground and worship. I'm going to show you how you can break loose from the destructive cycles that keep dragging you down. It is a point of honor to say, "By God's grace, it stops with me. I am going to set my family line on a whole new course for generations to come."

Here is a work sheet to help you think through how to do it—how to actually break the cycle. Understand that you may also need a group, a friend, or a counselor to guide you through the healing process.

BREAKING THE CYCLE WORK SHEET

Are you ready to ask God to break your cycle? Don't let this moment pass. You never know how long it will be until you have another opportunity like this one. If you let it pass, it could mean many years of continuing a destructive cycle. Let me recommend that you write your answers on a separate sheet of paper—it's cathartic. If you want, you can ceremonially burn your paper when you're done. Or you can download from ManAliveBook.com this same work sheet with blank lines to write on.

In any event, don't rush through it.

1. *Understand your baggage.* What are the repetitive and destructive sins that you struggle with?

2. *Get out of denial. Ask for help.* Share what you're going through with your group. You may need a Christian counselor to help you get to the bottom of it.

3. *Grieve what could have been.* This includes all the broken parts of your life, such as not having a father who was really involved in your life; a mother who didn't love you well; or alcoholism, abuse, or abandonment issues. What have you missed that is hurtful?

4. *Forgive those who have sinned against you.* This was Paul's urging when he wrote, "Make allowance for each other's faults, and forgive anyone who offends you. Remember, the Lord forgave you, so you must forgive others" (Colossians 3:13). Write down others' names and what you forgive.

5. *Repent for all the ways you have sinned against others.* Unless it's impossible, apologize personally and seek forgiveness.

(continued on the next page)

When necessary and if possible, make restitution. Write down the names of people you have sinned against and the actions you plan to take. Trust in this great Bible promise: "If we confess our sins to him, he is faithful and just to forgive us our sins and to cleanse us from all wickedness" (1 John 1:9).

6. *Ask the Holy Spirit to cleanse and transform you by His power.* The power of God is as close as your next thought. Our bodies are the temples of the Holy Spirit. He lives to intercede for us. "The Holy Spirit helps us in our weakness. For example, we don't know what God wants us to pray for. But the Holy Spirit prays for us with groanings that cannot be expressed in words" (Romans 8:26).

7. *Be patient.* A few men experience immediate and total deliverance from their destructive sin cycles. For most of us, however, mending takes time. And like cutting a piece of string in half, the sinful nature never completely goes away, so we must continue to live by the Spirit day by day.

THINKING AHEAD

If you completed your own inventory with the "Breaking the Cycle Work Sheet," I'll bet you're feeling pretty good right now. Even hopeful. And you should. God is pleased.

You're also probably wondering, *Will this last?*

The answer is "Yes, but the battle is not over." We didn't fall into these destructive cycles overnight, so in most cases they won't go away without a fight. Remember, you are in a lifelong battle with the world, the flesh, and the devil. So anytime you find yourself slipping back, revisit the work sheet and keep processing. It's a journey. Take the journey with a few Christian brothers who, like you, are serious about breaking free from the repetitive sins that keep dragging them down.

▪ ▪ ▪

Take the journey with a few Christian brothers who, like you, are serious about breaking free.

▪ ▪ ▪

In this chapter we've started to unpack how you can grow as a disciple by getting on top of the destructive things you don't want to do. In the next chapters we'll shift to going after the positive things you want to do.

Now it's time to talk things over with your group. If you still don't have a group, start one.

REFLECTION AND DISCUSSION QUESTIONS

1 What were your parents like? Did you have a good relationship with your father? with your mother? What did your parents do right?

2 How can the "Breaking the Cycle Work Sheet" (pages 102–104) process help you put a stop to any destructive behaviors that keep dragging you down?

3 The chapter says, "It's what you do next that counts" (page 98). As a result of reading this chapter, what are you planning to do next?

6

Soul Making

THE PRIMAL NEED: TO SATISFY MY
SOUL'S THIRST FOR TRANSCENDENCE,
AWE, AND COMMUNION

Years ago I heard a speech by businessman Walt Meloon, founder of Correct Craft, the boat manufacturing company that makes the world-famous Ski Nautique.

To be honest, I don't remember anything he said. But when the speech was over, he stood by the door vigorously shaking hands with everyone as they left. When it was my turn, he grabbed my hand with both of his, looked me square in the eye, and said passionately, "Isn't God good?"

That caught me off guard. Sure, I thought God was good, but not nearly as good as Walt evidently did. It crossed my mind that he could be faking his attitude, but if he was, he was a world-class liar. Walt seemed to know God in ways that satisfied him deeply.

I wondered what could make a man feel so vibrantly alive toward God, because most men don't, and at the time, I was one of them. But I wanted to be alive like that. The possibility intrigued me.

The problem is that most men know only enough about God to be disappointed with Him.

Take Terrell. He was raised in an overly strict religious home, where his parents wouldn't let him go to movies, to parties, or out on dates. As soon as he was on his own, he bitterly turned his back on anything that smacked of religion. If Terrell had heard Walt exclaim, "Isn't God good?" he would have laughed in his face.

> ■ ■ ■
>
> The problem is that most men know only enough about God to be disappointed with Him.
>
> ■ ■ ■

But that isn't the end of the story. Terrell is doing well with his young technology services company. But he still feels a powerful need for a spiritual something—he can't quite say what. He's exploring other religious practices. He goes fishing a lot. "Out there, in my boat, I feel peaceful. I feel close to something or Someone bigger than myself," he says. "That's as good as it gets, at least for now."

Or take Joel. When he walked into our morning Bible study a while back, he said his spiritual journey had come to a screeching halt. He said his soul felt dry as dust. He's plenty active in his little parish, but sometimes he feels like church is actually keeping him *away* from God. "I say yes whenever I'm asked to serve, but it doesn't really satisfy me spiritually. Is there something wrong with me?" he asked. Joel loves God, but he'll tell you that he misses the aliveness he felt as a new believer.

What's happened to Terrell and Joel lines up with a twenty-year-long trend. The Barna Group's "State of the Church" report shows that American men's satisfaction with church is waning in every category:

- ▦ attendance (down to 36 percent)
- ▦ serving (down to 18 percent)
- ▦ sharing their faith (down to 23 percent)
- ▦ believing the Bible (down to 33 percent)
- ▦ participation in adult education classes (down to a mere 13 percent)

As men withdraw from places of worship and from living like disciples, no wonder their souls feel dry!

There's a big, fat lie that's been going around ever since I can remember. It goes something like this: "You're a guy, and guys are just not as spiritually wired as their Christian wives or girlfriends." But from my own life, and after years of working with men, I know that's not true. I bet you know it too.

Men may be wired differently than women in many respects. But I promise you this: the deep, primal need of our souls to seek after God is *not* one of them! Every one of us has what we could call the God Instinct encoded in our DNA.

God loves men's souls. He loves to awaken, save, nurture, and revive men's souls. The soul is the part of you that is eternal—the immaterial, inward part that survives the death of the body. A man's soul (as much as a woman's) is made for communion, or spiritual union, with God in this life as well as the next.

■ ■ ■

God loves men's souls. He loves to awaken, save, nurture, and revive men's souls.

■ ■ ■

Yet millions of men today feel dry as dust inside, even though—shocking as this may sound—they really do love Christ.

You might be one.

If you know what it feels like to be so dry inside that you feel you could blow away, I think you're going to come away from this chapter refreshed, hopeful, and feeling alive deep down inside—maybe for the first time in a very long while.

PRIMAL FIRE

Contrary to what you might pick up at the movies or from the guys at the ballpark, men are driven by much deeper needs than food, sex, sports, and beer. That's because you and I have a soul. Our souls are made to long for communion with God.

In this chapter I'm going to show you what it means to live with an ache in your soul for something more, something outside yourself—and what God wants you to do about it.

I'd describe the primal need of a man's soul like this:

Every man has a deep need in his soul to experience transcendence and awe, for satisfying personal encounters with God. A man can dodge this need, and his soul may lay dormant for years. But sooner or later, he will long to satisfy the God-given thirst of his soul for communion with his Maker.

Do you remember the first time you felt this longing?

If you're willing to let it, this powerful primal need can draw you into a soul-filling experience that makes you want to shout, "I'm alive!"

Unfortunately, the last thing most men think about is taking care of their souls. That's understandable. We love getting things done in the physical world. And then there's the pressure to meet deadlines, pay bills, and keep wives and children happy. The one who would like to eat your soul—the devil—loves it when you're distracted and under pressure. That's because he knows what every great defensive coach knows: men under pressure make mistakes.

Most men today lead busy, overscheduled lives. It takes a toll. If I could make only one observation about how men are doing today, I would say that men are tired. And not just physically tired but also emotionally, relationally, and spiritually exhausted.

And that's when you're most vulnerable. That's when the

devil sinks his razor-sharp teeth into your soul. That's when the dominoes begin to fall.

First, you get caught up in the rat race. Then you start leading an unexamined life. Then you start letting your wife or girlfriend set the spiritual tone. Then you stop paying attention to the life of your soul. Finally, you wake up one day feeling spiritually dry. Empty. Basically, I've just described the slow process by which men abandon their inheritance as sons of God and end up living like spiritual orphans.

■ ■ ■

The main business
of God is
soul making.

■ ■ ■

But it doesn't have to be that way.

That's because the main business of God is soul making. How does that happen? How does a normal, average guy end up with a soul that is fully awake and alive to God?

THE BUSINESS OF SOUL MAKING

One night Robert and his girlfriend were lying on a blanket next to a pond. They were looking up into a clear, star-studded sky. Robert recalled, "Suddenly I was awestruck. An awareness of transcendence and eternal power crept over me. My heart raced. Nothing was said, but a slumbering soul was awakened inside me that night. Within a few minutes, I resumed my secular way of thinking and living, but the fuse had been lit. From then on a curiosity to know the truth about God was planted in my soul."

Every man has had, or will have, similar experiences—both before and after salvation. The God Instinct is like a sleeper cell in your soul with a secret activation code known only to God. When it's your time, deep calls to deep. God draws you in.

These awakening experiences with God tend to last only for a moment, although they can last for hours. They can be sought but not manufactured. They seem to be given, not earned. But they can be triggered anywhere, anytime.

Which of these situations brings back a memory of a God encounter for you?

- looking across the vastness of the Grand Canyon
- hearing a sermon when your adrenaline kicked in and you thought, *The preacher is talking directly to me!*
- listening to a special song
- staring at a work of art, such as Michelangelo's *David* or a ceramic handprint made by your child
- standing in the middle of a mountain stream with waders and a fly rod
- meditating in a holy place, whether it's Westminster Abbey or a country church
- gazing at the blazing beauty of a sunrise

- ■ pondering the wonder of Hubble Space Telescope pictures
- ■ studying the laws of physics or microbiology
- ■ surviving a near-death experience
- ■ experiencing life-altering events, like the birth of a child or the death of a parent
- ■ being confronted by devastation in the wake of your sins
- ■ looking intently into the Word of God

In these God moments, we palpably sense that He is touching our souls. Men describe it in different ways: a feeling of awe, an experience of transcendence, something wholly other, a sense of majesty, a feeling of gravity, an overpowering might, an awareness of something indescribably pure and holy, or the sensation of being immersed in the warmth of God's loving presence.

> ■ ■ ■
>
> The veil is pulled back, and for a moment, God fills the tabernacle of your soul.
>
> ■ ■ ■

You may tingle. Your breathing may become labored. Your heart may pound. You may experience an impulse to worship, a longing to know your Maker, or a desire for closeness and communion with God. You may be overwhelmed by an awareness of your own sinfulness. You may be consumed by an overwhelming desire to love God. You may feel compelled to fall, or like you're being knocked to your knees, or you may find yourself prostrate on the floor. Or you may experience all of these at once.

Whatever your unique experience might be, during these awakening encounters with God you become profoundly aware that He is the Creator and you are the creature. The veil is pulled back, and for a moment, God fills the tabernacle of your soul.

Here's an example from my life. One Sunday morning in an adult education class, Patsy and I sat in a circle of metal chairs with eight other couples. My eyes were staring at the terrazzo floor, daydreaming about the coming week. Dan, our leader, was talking, and then he read this passage from the Bible:

Husbands, love your wives, just as Christ loved the
church. (Ephesians 5:25, NIV)

Actually, he kept reading, but I don't remember anything after that. It felt like I had been Tasered. I hadn't been loving my wife at all. I had been treating Patsy like an asset. I was a taker.

My face flushed beet red, and I broke out in a sweat that drenched my clothes. My skin was on fire. My heart was pounding. I just knew that I had been found out! I just knew the leader had picked this verse to single me out. I just knew the whole class knew what a jerk I was. I just knew that everyone in that circle was now staring at me with judgment, disdain, and disgust. The humiliation was so complete that I couldn't find the courage to look up. I just kept staring at a spot on the floor.

Not until several minutes later did I realize that the class had moved on. Whatever was taking place was just between God and me. I had been found out, splayed, shattered, convicted, found guilty, and broken by the blow of a single verse.

■ ■ ■

There is no reason you cannot have regular soul-making encounters with God.

■ ■ ■

That's my first memory of the transforming power of God's Word. Today, I understand that my encounter is an example of how God transacts the business of soul making. In my case, the Holy Spirit used the teacher's reading of His Word to bring me under the conviction of sin. That conviction quickened a burning fire in my soul—for reconciliation with God.

God has an infinite and eternal interest in your soul. That's because everything besides your soul will one day cease to exist. And that's why Jesus asked, "What do you benefit if you gain the whole world but lose your own soul? Is anything worth more than your soul?" (Matthew 16:26).

Soul making is the main business of God, but you and I

also have a part. The apostle James stated it this way: "Come close to God, and God will come close to you" (James 4:8). There is no reason you cannot have regular soul-making encounters with God. I have them almost every day—some big, some small. As it turns out, getting close to God is not complicated. Ninety-nine percent of communion and loving God is showing up. Let me explain.

HANGING OUT WITH JESUS

Recently, I led my men's Bible study through a series called "Hanging Out with Jesus." It's named after one day in the lives of the sisters Martha and Mary—a story that might be familiar to you but one that most men don't pay much attention to. We should.

In the story, told in Luke 10:38–42, Martha comes off as the responsible one. She opened her home to Jesus for a dinner—a good deed. She took care of "all the preparations that had to be made" (verse 40, NIV).

The Greek word for "preparations" (or "serving" in the King James Version) is *diakonia,* part of the word family from which we get the word *deacon.* It is also the same *diakonia* that is the spiritual gift of serving. Obviously, serving is an important part of Christian life, and Martha excelled at it.

Mary, on the other hand, was content to sit at the feet of

Jesus "listening to what he said" (verse 39, NIV). The King James Version says simply that she "heard his word." The Greek for "word" is *logos*.

Was Mary goofing off while her sister worked? Martha thought so. She said to Jesus, "Lord, don't you care that my sister has left me to do the work [*diakoneo*] by myself? Tell her to help me!" (verse 40, NIV).

To her credit, Martha took her work seriously, but she was also missing her God moment. She was saying, in essence, "Tell Mary to leave the real presence of Jesus because I need help in the kitchen."

> ■ ■ ■
>
> Fill up in your personal relationship with Jesus first, then serve out of the overflow of your communion with Him.
>
> ■ ■ ■

Think about it from a historical perspective. After a four-hundred-year famine of God's Word (no prophets had spoken Scripture for that long), the Word (*logos*) had become flesh and was living among men and women. People living in darkness had seen a great light. God's promise to repay for the years the locusts had eaten was at hand. The empty nets were about to be filled.

But Martha thought the chores came first. The story says, "Martha was *distracted* by all the preparations" (verse 40, NIV, emphasis added).

Hosting a memorable evening meal for Jesus seemed like

such an opportunity to Martha. What wouldn't you give for such a moment? But the Bible says it was a distraction. Distractions often come disguised as opportunities. If it was true then, how much more true must it be today in a culture as busy as ours?

Jesus answered Martha's concern with sensitivity, but He didn't mince words either. Listen to what He said:

> Martha, Martha…you are worried and upset about many things, but only one thing is needed. Mary has chosen what is better, and it will not be taken away from her. (verses 41–42, NIV)

He was telling Martha, in essence, "There will always be work to do. It is better to spend time with Me."

The spirit of Martha is all about task, service, appearances, worry, and stress. By comparison, the spirit of Mary is all about relationship, communion, worship, truth, and closeness to God.

For Jesus, relationship is more important than task. In fact, the relationship *is* the task. Jesus did not say, "Come to me, all of you who are weary…*and I will give you more work to do.*" Instead, He said, "and you will find rest for your souls" (Matthew 11:28–29). Sure, service is important—we're saved *for* good works. But the lesson is to fill up in your personal relationship with Jesus first, then serve out of the overflow of your communion with Him. The Great Commandment, according to Jesus, is this:

> "You must love the LORD your God with all your heart, all your soul, and all your mind." This is the first and greatest commandment. (Matthew 22:37–38)

But for men who feel dry in their souls and distant from God, how is that even possible? The way of Mary will accomplish for us what the way of Martha will miss. Jesus is saying to us today, "Brothers, you are worried and upset about many things, but only one thing is needed."

First, be with God. The work can wait.

Mary first. There will be plenty of time for Martha.

YOUR BEING VERSUS DOING PROFILE

Let's morph the ancient Mary and Martha into a contemporary Mark and Martin. Are you more like a "Let's hang out" Mark or a "Let's get something done" Martin? Think through the following questions, then rate yourself as honestly as you can:

1. Do you think people who spend a lot of time in worship or devotions are goofing off?
   ❏ Rarely or Never
   ❏ Sometimes
   ❏ Often
   ❏ Always

2. Like Martha, do you confuse distractions with opportunities?
   ❏ Rarely or Never
   ❏ Sometimes
   ❏ Often
   ❏ Always

3. Do you allow obligations to come between you and your time with God?
   ❏ Rarely or Never
   ❏ Sometimes
   ❏ Often
   ❏ Always

4. Are you worried and upset about many things?
   ❏ Rarely or Never
   ❏ Sometimes

(continued on the next page)

❒ Often

❒ Always

5. Do you have so many responsibilities that you feel guilty relaxing with God?

❒ Rarely or Never

❒ Sometimes

❒ Often

❒ Always

6. When you do sit down to spend time with God—perhaps to read the Bible, pray, and meditate on the Scriptures—do you feel pressured to hurry up and get through it?

❒ Rarely or Never

❒ Sometimes

❒ Often

❒ Always

How did you do? For most men, hanging out with Jesus doesn't come naturally, does it? Our comfort zone is generally doing, not being. Yet any man who leads a powerful spiritual life will tell you this: without communion with God, a man can never satisfy his soul thirst.

A Guy's Guide to Hanging Out with Jesus

Jesus is the most fascinating man who ever lived. He is "the visible image of the invisible God" (Colossians 1:15), "the exact representation of his being" (Hebrews 1:3, NIV), "all the fullness of God in a human body" (Colossians 2:9). Jesus said, "The Father and I are one" (John 10:30) and "Anyone who has seen me has seen the Father" (John 14:9). So hanging out with Jesus is hanging out with God.

Even though blow-me-away experiences with God can't be manufactured, it's within your reach to have personal, consistent communion with God. Here are three priorities I recommend to every man:

1. Know About God, Know God

Mike believed in God but had always been content to keep the relationship intellectual. But during a personal crisis, God awakened Mike's soul and gave him an overwhelming desire to know Jesus personally. Suddenly he was consumed with a passion to not only know *about* God but to really know *Him*.

Perhaps you've heard of this distinction between knowing *about* God and knowing God. Authentic, vibrant faith is based on accurate knowledge *about* God, sure—but it's also based on personal experiences *with* God.

Let's call these, respectively, *theology for the head* (truth, knowledge) and *doxology for the heart* (spirit, communion). We need both. Both are forms of worship. We know this because John 4:24 says, "God is Spirit, so those who worship him must worship in spirit and in truth."

How does that happen? Since 1988 I've read through the Bible every year. Sometimes I follow a Bible reading plan (several plans are available on the Internet). Other times I read different versions of *The One Year Bible*.

■ ■ ■

Authentic, vibrant faith is based on accurate knowledge *about* God, sure—but it's also based on personal experiences *with* God.

■ ■ ■

I read the Bible for two reasons: to *know about* God and to experience *communion with* God. First and foremost, Christianity is a relationship with the Father, Jesus, and the Holy Spirit, who lavish their love on me. When I read the Bible, I am literally spending time with the living God. The Bible, along with prayer, is the gateway to communion with God. I also read the Bible for discipleship—to grow and mature in faith.

If you want to hang out with Jesus, the Bible is the place to start. A friend of mine, John Smith, asked, "What do you think would happen if I offered you ten million dollars to read the

Bible from cover to cover over the next year?" Of course you would read it. Well, it's worth a lot more than ten million dollars. Everything Jesus knew as a man is in there. He said, "I have told you everything the Father told me" (John 15:15). With such an encyclopedic treasure trove of His words—34,450 to be exact—why wouldn't we want to start there?

Bible reading works best when it's a habit with a regular time and place. I like early mornings in a favorite chair, and I shoot for five days a week. How long? Some guys spend fifteen minutes a day; some spend two hours—it's completely up to you. (For more, you can read a free article called "How to Have a Consistent Quiet Time" at ManAliveBook.com.)

Spending time to know God and know about God is central to your discipleship—and it comes with a huge promise. Jesus put it this way: "You are truly my disciples if you remain faithful to my teachings. And you will know the truth, and the truth will set you free" (John 8:31–32). We've all wondered why Christians "stray." It's because they don't invest themselves in remaining faithful to the teachings of Jesus.

2. LEAVE ROOM FOR MYSTERY

On a recent January 1, I read the Creation account in Genesis 1 and said out loud (to be honest, squealed like a girl), "Mystery abounds!" I then wrote *Mystery abounds!* at the bottom of the page.

Also, I decided to put the initials *MA* at the bottom of any page on which I found something that was mysterious, that seemed hard to understand, or that raised a question. Can you guess how many pages I initialed that year?

All of them.

Mystery, which is truth beyond human understanding, is built into the deal. God declares,

> As the heavens are higher than the earth,
>   so are my ways higher than your ways
>   and my thoughts than your thoughts.
>   (Isaiah 55:9, NIV)

We get this. We've all had to hold back information from someone we didn't think could handle it.

Part of communion is trusting—and loving—the mystery of God. We must often squint at the beauty of God's holiness through a thick veil of human limitation.

But what about all the questions you have for and about God that are unanswered?

Allow me to show you something. I'm going to ask you to bow your head, close your eyes, and fold your hands in prayer. Then I want you to think about what your posture is trying to communicate to God.

Assume this prayer posture for a count of five. I'll wait...

Okay, so what's your answer? If you said, "He is the infinite God and I'm just me," or simply "Humility," you'd be right. We don't come to God as equals. We come to Him with awe and humility. Some things in this life we'll never understand—and we were never meant to.

> ▪ ▪ ▪
>
> Never want a God you can fully explain.
>
> ▪ ▪ ▪

I'd take it even further: never want a God you can fully explain.

3. TAKE YOUR TIME

A business colleague and I were in New York City. Whenever I'm there, I try to take in the Monet collection at the Metropolitan Museum of Art. As we left for the airport, I asked my friend if he wanted to catch the Monets.

He said, "I'm in," but we were tight on time. So we asked the cab driver to wait outside the museum while we dashed in for ten minutes with Monet. Almost as soon as we arrived, we had to turn around and brisk-walk back to our waiting cab.

Of course, you can't really get Monet by treating his paintings like fast food. Ten minutes isn't enough to really appreciate the depth, color, texture, and mood that are there. You have to stand, be quiet, and wait. And then, suddenly, it hits you.

It's the same with communion with God. You can't really experience transcendence and awe unless you slow down and quiet yourself.

I define *hang time* as anything that nurtures your soul with a sense of the power and presence of Jesus. It can be quiet times, Bible reading, small groups, Bible studies, conversations about God, contemplative moments, singing in church, listening to music in your car, listening to a sermon, watching a sunrise, or worshiping while hammering new shingles onto a widow's roof.

Remember, it's a Person you're after, not a task to check off your to-do list.

GAME CHANGER

In this chapter you've seen how raw and personal our primal need for transcendence, awe, and communion can be. There are so many things that hold us back, but getting it right is pretty simple. That's because the main business of God is soul making. He wants communion with us far more than we do with Him. Mostly, it's about showing up and hanging out.

> ■ ■ ■
> Be sure to build time for hanging out with Jesus into your schedule.
> ■ ■ ■

If there isn't "anything worth more than your soul," if the greatest commandment is "to love the Lord your God," and if "only one thing is needed," then shouldn't communion be your top priority?

Be sure to build time for hanging out with Jesus into your schedule. It's something that men who lead powerful, transformed lives do differently than their lukewarm counterparts. For men who desperately want to be fully alive, it's a game changer.

REFLECTION AND DISCUSSION QUESTIONS

1 In this chapter, you read about how God awakened Robert's soul and also how He ignited a fire in my soul. What is your first recollection of God's awakening your soul? Which of the bulleted triggers (pages 115–116) in the section "The Business of Soul Making" makes you feel closest to God, and why?

2 What is the difference between the spirit of Martha and the spirit of Mary? Where do you fall in the spectrum between these two?

3 If it's true that you can experience soul-making encounters with God just by showing up, what would you like to do differently?

7

TO LOVE AND BE LOVED

THE PRIMAL NEED: TO LOVE AND BE LOVED WITHOUT RESERVATION

John headed home after work thinking it was just another ordinary day. But it wasn't, and John would never forget what happened next.

He opened the door to a dark house.

"Hello?" he called. No answer. Concerned, he went into the kitchen, where he found a note from his wife. It read, *We just can't take it anymore. We're leaving. I'm taking the kids and we're going back home. I'm sorry.*

John's heart sank. He didn't know what to think, what to do. He pounded the kitchen counter in anger, then he began to sob. Those emotions soon gave way to an overwhelming sense of fear—fear of being alone, of losing his family, of losing the life he had worked so hard to build.

■ ■ ■

I never saw it coming.

■ ■ ■

Standing there in his darkened house, John tried to figure out where he had gone wrong. How could his life have come to this? That night and for days after, all he could think was, *I never saw it coming.*

John's story is extreme, but I've known hundreds of men facing or heading toward similar situations. In fact, a huge percentage of men I talk to admit that their most important relationships are not working. But too many keep fumbling along until it's too late.

Are we doomed to end up in a dark house like John, with no clue about what just hit us?

No way! There's a whole other side to the story.

WHAT DO MEN WANT?

Despite what you see in the headlines and hear on the talk shows, men *are* made for relationships. I'd even go so far as to say that, for a man, relationships trump everything else. Just ask a young father languishing in prison or a soldier far from home what's most important. Every man I've ever talked to—and that includes teenagers, bachelors, divorced men, grandfathers, and more—sincerely wants to have strong, healthy, loving relationships.

■ ■ ■

Despite what you see in the headlines and hear on the talk shows, men *are* made for relationships.

■ ■ ■

And a man is also wired to want a special relationship—a soul mate he can share his deepest thoughts and dreams with and still feel safe.

I would describe a man's primal need in this area like this:

Every man feels a deep, powerful need to nurture and be nurtured, to love and be loved without reservation, to take care of someone, and to feel at least one person really knows him for who he is and loves him anyway. Even if a man never marries or has children, this need is just as primal— it just gets satisfied differently. Most men, however, feel like they have a handicap when it comes to relationships.

Why do men feel so handicapped when it comes to relationships? It might be because we haven't grown up paying attention to how relationships really work. Once we marry and start a family, we get distracted. We don't invest time in meaningful conversations. When conflicts arise, we withdraw, unsure of how to make things better. Or like John, we simply stop minding the store.

Over and over, men ask me these same questions: "What can I do to make her happy?" "How can I raise godly kids?" and "How can I have friendships that go deeper than trading jokes?"

Their hearts are in the right place, but they're frustrated at the practical level.

How about you? Do you feel handicapped in your most important relationships?

The good news of this chapter is not just that men are made for love but also that our shortcomings are not fatal. That's because love is a skill that can be learned and improved. You can bring your *capabilities* up to par with your *intentions.*

But is it too late for John? Let's go back and check on him.

A YELLOW TIE AND TWO PAIRS OF SOCKS

A few days after his big shock, John found himself sitting in the office of a marriage counselor bawling his eyes out. He was crushed, but he was also desperate for answers.

At the end of the session, the counselor reached into his desk drawer. "Here," he said, passing a business card to John. "This will do you more good than anything." The card directed John to a Friday morning men's Bible study.

As he walked away, John thought, *A Bible study? Are you kidding me? I don't need a Bible study. I need you to fix my marriage. I want my family back!*

But on Friday morning he forced himself out of bed. As he walked into a room full of strangers, he was overcome by embarrassment and shame. Yet instead of feeling judged, he found men who cared, listened, and related to his pain. At first John was stiff as a board. But after a few meetings he began to thaw out and, before long, started to open up and share his sins and sorrows.

Eventually his family moved back home, but John's many mistakes and sins had turned his wife's heart cold as ice. Even his children sided against him. He saw his next five birthdays come and go without a card or even a verbal acknowledgment of the day. But he was determined to do what it took to win his family back.

While his home life continued to flounder, John's faith flourished. His group continued to listen, mentor, pray, and sometimes weep with him. As John studied God's Word, he began to understand what it means to be a godly man, husband, and father. He began to grasp the power of loving unconditionally. He learned how to love himself and build honorable relationships with others. He started to pray for his wife and children. He began to try to change the spiritual climate in his home.

One evening John called a family meeting. He announced that he was taking over the family finances and that they would start living on a budget.

That decision proved to be a turning point. His wife and children began to respond to John's new way of loving and leading. His wife started to give him an occasional smile or kind word.

One day she gave him an unsolicited hug.

Three months later, on his birthday, John received a text from his wife. It said, "Happy birthday!" John was shocked and delighted. When he arrived home, his wife followed him into their bedroom. There on a chair sat a present. She giggled at his surprise. As he opened the gift, she kept repeating, "If you don't like it, you can take it back."

John ripped off the wrapping paper and opened the box to find a yellow tie and two pairs of socks. Somehow his wife had gotten the idea he wanted a yellow tie. John hadn't worn a tie in years! His first thought was to take her up on her offer and exchange it. But just as quickly the Holy Spirit gave him the wisdom to say, "I love my yellow tie!"

And then he put it on.

This was no ordinary yellow tie, he realized. This was a sign of forgiveness and new beginnings. This was proof of God's grace.

Today, John is so glad that he learned to love God's way. Was his comeback road a tough one? Sure. For seven long years he gave love without getting much in return. But during that time God had been at work, transforming his life, his marriage, and his family.

Your situation may not have deteriorated to the same ex-

■ ■ ■

But just as quickly the Holy Spirit gave him the wisdom to say, "I love my yellow tie!"

■ ■ ■

tent. I sincerely hope not. But if a situation as desp
can be redeemed, how much more likely is it that the c
you face today can also be redeemed?

IF YOU CAN CHOOSE ONLY
ONE WORD

Let's face it—relationships are messy. But as a friend says, "Relationships are messes worth making."

If we didn't have relationship problems, the Bible could be a lot shorter—maybe 80 percent shorter. The Bible clearly shows us God's will for how we relate to spouses, children, extended family, neighbors, employers, coworkers, friends, and even enemies. If our most important mission as disciples of Jesus is to be in right relationship with God, our second most important mission is to be in right relationship with each other.

Loving others proves we are disciples. Jesus said:

A new command I give you: Love one another. As I
have loved you, so you must love one another. By this
all men will know that you are my disciples, if you love
one another. (John 13:34–35, NIV)

Cut the Bible and it bleeds neighbor love. In fact, the Bible declares that loving others is the essence of Scripture.

...med up in this one command:

...urself." (Galatians 5:14)

...neback story demonstrates a power-

...in the world that can be resisted, the

...ove. If you can choose only one word

to live by, let it be ... ove is the glue that will hold us together and the oil that will keep us from rubbing each other raw.

For the rest of this chapter I'm going to show you how to turn inventory into cash. Here are the best of the best, most practical love-in-action ideas I've accumulated for the two most important relationships most men will ever have: with a woman and with a child.

You'll notice that the focus is on what you give, not on what you get. That's because men are to be the spiritual leaders. Leaders give before they receive. And I guarantee that if you lead in love, your wife and children and everyone else important to you will respond in kind.

HOW TO REALLY LOVE A WOMAN

God designed marriage to be the most personal relationship in all creation. Marriage is the mysterious fusion of two separate lives into what the Bible calls "one flesh" (Genesis 2:24, NIV). In no other relationship do two people exchange for-better-or-worse vows, become one, make babies, build a home together, share a bed, see each other naked, and become soul mates. When a marriage works, everything works.

At the same time, marriage is the most difficult relationship. I've discovered that if you put men's marriage problems in one stack and *all* their other problems in a second stack, the first stack is higher. Easily the number one problem men face is that their marriages are not working the way God designed them to work. And to make matters worse, the institution of marriage itself is under assault in our culture.

> ▪ ▪ ▪
>
> The number one problem men face is that their marriages are not working the way God designed them to work.
>
> ▪ ▪ ▪

If there's one relationship where you want transformation, this is it. If there's one relationship in which you want to experience unconditional love, this is it. When it comes to marriage, what do men who have strong marriages do differently than those who don't?

Here are ten practical love-is-what-love-does ways to show your love.

1. PRAY WITH YOUR WIFE

Shaun from Bozeman, Montana, asked his men's group, "How many of you pray with your wives?" Only one of the eight men

said that he did. They started holding each other accountable.
Here's what Shaun said about it a year later:

> The benefits when we are obedient in this area are
> amazing. Here are some comments from the men
> about what happens when they pray with their wives
> on a consistent basis:
> - ■ "I feel a closeness to my wife that wasn't
>   there before."
> - ■ "Communication between us is
>   better."
> - ■ "The petty things are just not a big
>   deal anymore."
>
> And I'll tell you this, it's pretty hard to be upset
> with your wife or to be arguing and still come before
> God with a clean heart. It forces us to communicate
> and humble ourselves with each other before we do
> something as intimate as praying together. It just
> permeates through the rest of your family and day.

Ask your wife if you can take some time each day to pray
together. Patsy and I always start the day with prayer for one to
three minutes, and then we pray again when we're together for
dinner.

2. Pray for Your Wife

Not long ago I wrote a book called *The Marriage Prayer* with David Delk. The book is titled after a very specific sixty-eight-word prayer that we believe captures the essence of what the Bible teaches on marriage.

One day, a few months after I had started praying the marriage prayer myself, I was settled into my favorite chair and deep into a book when I saw Patsy walking by with the trash. I literally leaped out of my chair and said, "Here, let me get that for you."

Immediately I stopped. *What just happened here?* I wondered, since I was pretty sure I had never done that before!

And then a phrase from the marriage prayer popped into my mind: "I want to hear her, cherish her, and serve her—so she would love You more and we can bring You glory."

> "I want to hear her, cherish her, and serve her."

This prayer has also been transforming for other men. One man said he started putting his empty Splenda packets in the trash instead of leaving them on the counter. You have to start somewhere.

Here's the whole marriage prayer:

Father, I said, "Till death do us part"—I want to mean it.
Help me to love You more than her,

and her more than anyone or anything else.
Help me bring her into Your presence today.
Make us one, like You are three-in-one.
I want to hear her, cherish her, and serve her—
So she would love You more and
we can bring You glory. Amen.

Think about this: you are likely the only person in the whole world who will remember to regularly pray for your mate. Tear out or copy this prayer, pray it every day for your wife, and watch God work. Learn more about the Marriage Prayer—including a version for a wife to pray—at ManAlive Book.com.

3. SPEND TIME WITH HER ALONE

How we spend our time reveals what is really important to us. Successful couples spend time together. They develop shared interests, like bowling, reading, hiking, Bible studies, board games, or walking around the neighborhood. Patsy and I have always kept a weekly date night as a top priority.

Early in our marriage, I started hanging out at the table after dinner for about twenty minutes just to be with Patsy. We've done this for decades. A few years ago I also started rubbing her feet with lotion as we talk. I can guarantee you who she'll say is her best friend!

4. Listen to Her Deeply Without Giving an Overly Quick Reply

Communication invariably shows up as the number one problem in marriage surveys. And the greatest weakness in communication with our mates is the problem of giving an overly quick reply. We attach high value to our mates when we listen sincerely and patiently to each other. Listening deeply requires that we don't respond too quickly, don't criticize, and don't give advice unless the other person asks for it. (Everyone dreads being "fixed.") Listening lubricates marriage and cuts down on friction.

5. Touch Her

Successful couples touch each other. They hug, squeeze, embrace, pat, hold hands, put their arms around each other, and sit close enough to touch when watching television. Nonsexual touching leads to genuine intimacy. Touching her is like recharging her battery.

6. Accept Her Unconditionally

Happy wives don't feel like they have to perform to be loved. They don't feel like they will be rejected if they don't meet a set of standards. For Pete's sake, if your wife has fat ankles, don't say something stupid like "Why don't you do ankle exercises?" Jesus accepts each of us "just as I am," as the old hymn says, and smart mates accept each other as is too. Intimacy means that I know who you are at the deepest level and I accept you.

7. ENCOURAGE HER WITH WORDS

Your mate has an emotional bank account into which you make deposits and from which you make withdrawals. If you're grumpy when you get home from work, you are making a withdrawal from her account. When you encourage your spouse when she feels down, you are making a deposit. (Make sure to keep track of the account balance!)

> ■ ■ ■
>
> Encouragement is the food of the heart, and every heart is a hungry heart.
>
> ■ ■ ■

We all need to be lifted up when we feel blue, but the most successful couples go one step further—they create a positive environment. They verbally affirm each other at every opportunity. They try to catch each other doing things right. They pass along compliments others make about their mate. They never pass up an opportunity to express appreciation: "I love the way you fix your hair." "That was a great dinner." "I love having you for my wife." "Thank you for running such a smooth home."

Encouragement is the food of the heart, and every heart is a hungry heart.

8. Take Care of Her Financially

Money problems create more stress on a marriage than any other outside threat. Here is the money issue in a nutshell: is it right to spend so much on a lifestyle today that your wife would be forced into panic mode if you were not around anymore? Successful couples have resolved to live within their means. They do not live so high today that they fail to provide for retirement and premature death.

9. Laugh with Her

The antidote to boredom in marriage is lively humor. If your partner says something even remotely funny, laugh! Keep track of what brings a smile to her face and what makes her laugh till her sides hurt. If neither one of you is funny, watch funny movies and make some funny friends.

10. After God but Before All Others, Make Your Wife Your Top Priority

Once I called three friends to pray for a difficult challenge I faced the next day. One week later I called each of them to let them know how it turned out. "Oh yeah," every one of them said, "I've been meaning to call you."

Sure.

Men, you and your wife are the only two people who are really in this thing together. Everyone else will phase in and out of your lives—even your children. One day soon the party will be over and all your golfing buddies will have moved to Florida to live in little condominium pods and drive around on streets made for golf carts. And there will be only two rocking chairs sitting side by side. One for you, and one for her.

Doesn't it make sense to invest today in the person who will be sitting next to you then? Be your wife's best friend.

HOW TO REALLY LOVE A CHILD

Nothing is more precious to a man than his children. If your children are doing well, all your other problems will fit into a thimble.

Raising godly kids today takes intentionality. That means the right amount of structure, time, prayers, hugs, encouraging words, and verbal affection. My own children are grown now. I know I did a lot of things wrong, but here are ten practical love-in-action things I did right for you to consider. Remember, love is what love does.

> ■ ■ ■
>
> If your children are doing well, all your other problems will fit into a thimble.
>
> ■ ■ ■

1. PAY YOUR CHILDREN TO READ THE BIBLE

Christian parents want their children to grow up and stay true to faith in Jesus. And nothing has more potential to transform our children into faithful followers than reading God's Word. But it won't happen by itself.

Patsy and I had an unconventional idea about this. When our kids were about twelve and nine, we decided to pay them to read the Bible. We told them, "If you will read five minutes a day for twenty-five or more days in a month, we'll give you the money to buy whatever CD you want. You can use a Bible devotional if you want." I thought I detected a yawn.

> ■ ■ ■
>
> Paying our kids to read the Bible was the single best thing we ever did for our children's faith.
>
> ■ ■ ■

Then we added, "And if you read twenty-five days for ten out of twelve months, we will pay you $250." Suddenly their eyes lit up!

Finally we said, "But if you read twenty-five days or more a month for all twelve months, we will double that and pay you $500." That really got their attention!

Our kids made monthly calendars, taped them to their

mirrors, and made an X through each day they read. We put them on the honor system and even gave them the ability to make up missed days.

Was that bribery? I don't know. All I know is that our kids always did their daily devotions, their friends didn't, our kids still do, and they both love Jesus. Paying our kids to read the Bible was the single best thing we ever did for our children's faith.

If you try this, just make sure to focus on shaping their hearts and not controlling their behavior. It worked for us because we raised our children in a grace-based home rather than a performance-based home. Don't let it become legalistic.

2. Lead Your Children in Family Devotions

Three or four days a week during the school year, we had a fifteen-minute family devotion. We timed them so the kids wouldn't be late for school. I usually started with a life situation—something in the neighborhood, from the newspaper, or a school situation. Then I read a Scripture passage that applied. We finished with each of us saying a short prayer. To make the prayers more than "Let us have a good day," we prayed for someone in need each time. We always broke for the summer because everyone was on a different sleep schedule.

3. Establish Work Boundaries

Since family was my highest value from the beginning, I set up some rules: quit work no later than 6:00 p.m. every day, don't take work home, and don't work weekends. To help me not take work home, during my evening commute I'd let my mind process what I'd been doing during the workday until I went over a creek about a mile from our home. Then I would put everything into a mental briefcase and toss it into the creek. That gave me a couple of minutes to prepare to greet my family. When I started traveling, we decided as a family that I could travel up to five nights a month—no more.

If you want to lead a balanced life, decide how many hours you want to work and stick to your guns. Put work appointments on your calendar in pencil, but put your family commitments in pen. If you don't set your own boundaries, someone will set them for you. Love is time, and time is love.

4. Make Your Family Your Number One Ministry

A tornado ripped through our church building. The call went out for volunteers to help clean up on Saturday. But my son had a game that day, and I thought the game was a higher priority. So I went to the game instead of joining the work team. On Sunday the volunteers were asked to stand and be thanked publicly. I felt guilt and shame for not having been there with them—even though it quickly went away.

Without intending to do so, churches can put pressure on you to serve others to the neglect of your own family. You know this is true, because you have felt this pressure. But what's your response going to be?

No one else cares about your family like you do. You have to be strong, and you have to set boundaries. No one else can, or should, take responsibility to disciple your family. That one's on you. Your most important small group, prayer group, fellowship group, discipleship group, and ministry is your family. Until you get this right, you really shouldn't be doing ministry anywhere else.

> ■ ■ ■
>
> Your most important small group, prayer group, fellowship group, discipleship group, and ministry is your family.
>
> ■ ■ ■

The greatest need of our children is for encouragement. How do I know that? Because Colossians 3:21 says, "Fathers, do not aggravate your children, or they will become discouraged." So what's the opposite of to *discourage*? It's to *encourage*.

I've seen dads discourage their kids in two important ways. First, a *lack of involvement*. Many dads have no idea what their kids are doing after school, who their friends are, what classes they're struggling with, or even what classes their kids are taking. Kids *want* their dads involved.

Second, *too much structure.* At the other extreme a lot of dads clamp down too rigidly on things like hair, clothing, makeup, and dating. The tendency is to provide too much freedom where there should be involvement, and too much structure where there should be freedom. For example, telling your kids they can't get their ears pierced, but then letting them go see any movies they want.

So what's the right approach? A grace-based home with clear boundaries. We didn't worry one minute when our son wanted to grow his hair long and bleach it (it turned orange!). You have to pick your battles carefully. You can raise your children under grace or law, but grace is better. If you raise them under too much law they may not want to spend much time with you once they're on their own.

5. Spend Time with and Date Your Children

When our kids were young, we played board games after dinner. I endured endless, mind-numbing repetitions of Candy Land and Chutes and Ladders—games that require the IQ of a goldfish. During those same years, I kept them every Saturday morning so Patsy could run errands. Later, I drove them to school for several years. Once they hit the teens, I started taking one child out every Tuesday for a dinner date and something fun, like ice cream, go-carts, or the mall. Looking back, those were the best, and almost only, one-on-one times we had. If you're not intentional about this, a whole year can go by without your sharing a single deep conversation with your kids.

6. Pray for and Encourage Your Children with Words Every Day

I quickly realized that my wife and I were probably the only ones who would intentionally pray in specifics for our kids every day. So I made up a list of things to pray over—their salvation, growth, integrity, work ethic, spirituality, protection, future mates, and so on. I don't think it's a coincidence that all those specifics we prayed for are today a reality.

I made it a goal to tell each of my children every day "I love you and I'm proud of you"—words I didn't hear growing up, which still affects me today. Of course, I didn't hit every day, but I sure came close! Do it as much as you can. There's biblical precedent for this: At both the baptism of Jesus and the transfiguration, God spoke and said, "You are my dearly loved Son, and you bring me great joy." In other words, "I love him and I'm proud of him."

7. Attend As Many of Your Children's Activities As Possible

Perhaps because of my own experience with my parents not attending my games, I decided from the start that I would never miss a recital or a game. And I never did. Fortunately, my work allowed that flexibility. One of my greatest joys came the day my son said, "Dad, I don't know what I want to do, but whatever it is, I want a career that lets me attend my kids' games like you attended mine."

8. Eat Dinner Together

The dinner table is more than food—a lot more. It can be the medium that allows families to transfer spiritual and moral values from one generation to the next. There's a lot of research to support this, and we knew it. So we worked around school activities. We didn't answer the phone during dinner. We made eating dinner together a priority.

That's not likely to happen for you every night without fail, but at least don't make choices that preclude it.

9. Expose Your Children to Ministry

We participated as a family in many of the ministry opportunities offered by our church. In fact, we selected ministries precisely because we could include our children, such as housing visiting missionaries and delivering Thanksgiving meals. Our kids participated in the youth groups, but we never thought that we had delegated our parenting to the paid professionals. When they were older, our kids went without us to youth camps and on mission trips. That helped them build confidence in their own faith.

10. Make Your Children Responsible to Attend Church

For much the same reasons that it would be foolish to let your kids skip school, it would be foolish to let them skip church. When kids are preteens, they will freely go to church if you go. When our kids were teens, though, we experienced resistance.

■ ■ ■

We transferred responsibility for attending church to our kids.

■ ■ ■

They were "too tired to go to church" after being out on Saturday night. And that's when my wife came up with an ingenious idea. Rather than do battle every Sunday morning, we transferred responsibility for attending church to them. If they were too tired to attend church, they could sleep in and skip church, but then the following Saturday night they needed to stay home so they wouldn't be so tired. Guess how many times that happened? That's right. Once.

These ten love-in-action ideas paid a huge dividend in our family. When our daughter was six, I helped her pray to receive Jesus. Two years later, she helped our four-year-old son pray to receive Jesus. And they've never looked back.

You Hold an Awesome Power

Right now, people in your life—your wife or girlfriend, your kids, your parents, your closest friends—desperately need to know that someone loves them as they are. They yearn for someone who will overlook their faults, forgive their sins, and love them without reserve. They hunger for someone who delights in and believes in them. They thirst for someone who thinks they're great—who thinks the best of their motives. Whether they can articulate it or not, they long for someone who will make them feel safe.

You are God's designated solution. Are you willing to make the first move...and keep on making it?

Challenge yourself to risk everything to be a vessel of God's love. It will transform your relationships, starting at home. Use the *love* word indis-

■ ■ ■

You are God's designated solution.

■ ■ ■

criminately, even recklessly. Ask God to empower you to be uninhibited in love.

Jesus proved it's true: there's nothing more powerful in this world than a man who will love without reservation.

REFLECTION AND DISCUSSION QUESTIONS

1 Right now, people in your life desperately need to know that you love them as they are. Who are these people, and to the extent you feel comfortable in sharing about it, what are the issues preventing you from loving them without reservation?

2 Right now, you, too, desperately need to be loved. Maybe the woman you love has closed off her spirit to you or your child blames you for something. As far as it is up to you, how can you bring that relationship back to biblical love?

3 Which of the practical love-in-action ideas in this chapter struck a chord with you? Why? Which ideas do you plan to implement?

8

How a Man Makes His Mark

The primal need: To make a contribution and leave the world a better place

Even though Bill has been unemployed for more than a year and can barely make ends meet, he's still holding out. He doesn't want just any job. He wants to be part of something that is making a difference in the world.

Steve is at the other end of the spectrum. "I've achieved everything I wanted," he told me recently. "I have a luxury home, a beautiful wife, perfect kids, a high-powered job, and lots of money. Not long ago I deposited a $100,000 check. But that evening, when my wife and I had a drink to celebrate, I was downcast. I realized something was missing."

His wife tried to help him figure out what it was. "What exactly do you want?" she asked him.

All Steve could tell her was, "I don't know."

Whether a man is just trying to survive or he's made it and feels the excruciating emptiness of mere success, he's been wired by God to crave something more. All of us have been.

This craving is not about gaining prestige, wielding power, or winning the admiration of others. Those are the illusions of youth.

The craving is different from our drive to provide for our families or to achieve financial security—as good and important as those things are. It's different from knowing you're a Christian. It even goes beyond knowing that your life has a purpose, that your life is not random (remember chapter 4?).

The craving I'm talking about is a man's innate and powerful need for significance. I would describe this seventh primal need like this:

> *Every man feels a deep need to make a difference, to make his life count, and to leave the world a better place. Yet in the crush of daily duties, this powerful need often gets misdirected or ignored.*

No inner need has a stronger pull for men than our need for a life that matters. It starts out like a tropical storm when we're young, and by midlife it intensifies into a category 5 hurricane. And it *never* goes away. It's like a giant turbine that's always humming in the background.

One of the primary determiners of a man's happiness is how and whether he satisfies this craving. Not happy here, not happy anywhere. If a man has a difficult marriage, he can compartmentalize it. But if a man doesn't think his life is making any difference, his misery will spill over and affect everything.

No man wants to be a shooting star that streaks across the sky one night and then disappears. We all want our lives to count. Apple founder Steve Jobs put it well when he famously said, "We're here to make a dent in the universe."

▪ ▪ ▪

No inner need has a stronger pull for men than our need for a life that matters.

▪ ▪ ▪

Unfortunately, as Oliver Wendell Holmes once said, most people go to their graves with their best music still inside them. In my experience, that shocking statement applies especially in the area of significance—and not just for non-Christian men but for Christian men too. I'd say 90 percent of Christian men don't go much further than professing faith. They're saved but stuck—inside the stadium but not in the game. Their lives seem pointless, and they hate it.

How would you describe your own need in this area? Would you say you are content with the direction and meaning of your life? Or would you say you're feeling something far short of contentment?

In this chapter I'm going to show you how to find a life of significance. You were created to make a dent in the universe. So go get it!

MADE FOR A SPECIFIC MISSION

A friend of mine with a large boat was talking to a diesel mechanic. The mechanic asked, "When do you use your onboard generator?"

My friend answered, "Oh, we try to use it as little as possible, mostly for the refrigerator."

The mechanic said, "That's all wrong. Your generator is looking for a load. People think they're saving their generators by not using them. But they actually perform better and last longer when you put a load on them."

Men are like that too—we're designed to perform best and last longer when we have a load on us. And the kind of load that will energize a man, not drag him down year after year, is one that produces results of lasting value. Jesus put it this way: "When you produce much fruit, you are my true disciples. This brings great glory to my Father" (John 15:8). By "fruit," Jesus meant good works, and as you can see, bearing fruit is at the heart of authentic discipleship. Ephesians 2:8–10 says that we are saved *by* faith, *not* works—but it also goes on to say that we are saved *for* works.

> ■ ■ ■
>
> Men are designed to perform best and last longer when we have a load on us.
>
> ■ ■ ■

And it's not just bearing fruit in a general way. God has a specific plan for your life as unique as your fingerprint. It's a program of service especially for you. It's your personal mission:

> We are God's masterpiece. He has created us anew in
> Christ Jesus, so we can do the good things he planned
> for us long ago. (Ephesians 2:10)

The stunning idea that God created you and me for a program of service can really stop a man in his tracks. Why? Because once we realize that God has a custom-made plan for us to make a lasting contribution, we can stop chasing counterfeits to satisfy our craving. This is the secret of significance: we will feel most significant, alive, and happy when we are doing what God created us to do.

It makes sense. How happy would an eagle be if he couldn't fly? Or a lion if he couldn't roar?

Two Ways to Make Your Mark

Not long ago a man excitedly sent me an e-mail about his sense of calling to lead a men's small group. He wrote, "My career is what I'm *paid* to do, but my calling is what I'm *made* to do!"

Sounds good, doesn't it?

Unfortunately, it's bad theology. God makes no distinction between *sacred* and *secular*. For Christians, all of life is spiritual.

God gives all of us two kinds of tasks that will make a difference in the world and leave a legacy for eternity. The first are tasks that build Christ's kingdom and fulfill the Great Commission. The second are tasks that take care of creation—that is, the natural world, including everything and everyone in it. When we tend to these tasks, we fulfill what's often called the Creation Mandate.

■ ■ ■

For Christians, all of life is spiritual.

■ ■ ■

We'll spell this out in more detail in the next section. But here's the important thing: both are spiritual.

The Great Commission includes all things *vertical* (or *eternal*)—redeeming people by connecting them with God.

The Creation Mandate includes all things *horizontal* (or *temporal*)—redeeming the world by raising families, taking on productive work, and serving others for the greater good.

Often we'll be doing both tasks at once, like doing our horizontal work so well that it creates vertical curiosity about what makes us tick. Think of these two kinds of tasks as keys that unlock a life of significance for a man and allow him to make a contribution that will far outlast his years on earth.

Let's take them one at a time.

TAKING CARE OF CREATION

God loves His world. His Creation Mandate to take care of the world, which the Bible reveals starting in Genesis 1:27–28, is an important way He expresses that love:

> So God created human beings in his own image.
>> In the image of God he created them;
>> male and female he created them.
>
> Then God blessed them and said, "Be fruitful and multiply. Fill the earth and govern it. Reign over the fish in the sea, the birds in the sky, and all the animals that scurry along the ground.

The Creation Mandate is why we marry, raise families, strive for justice, build careers, participate as citizens, feed the poor, shelter the homeless, and volunteer.

Most of us will spend the vast majority of our time living out this care for creation. For example, easily half of our waking hours will be spent working (if you include getting ready and drive time). Typically, the rest goes to family, sports, recreation, entertainment, chores, and service.

But does that mean we have no opportunity to build the kingdom of God? Not at all.

I'll give you an example. Tim is a high school math teacher who is doing what he always wanted to do—teach math. But not long after he started his career in education, he noticed two problems. "First, my students were coming to class with problems that math can't solve," he told me. "Second, the Christian teachers in my school didn't know each other. God has given me a vision to address these two issues."

And then he said something I'll never forget. "I'm an ordained math teacher."

Yes! That's it exactly. Whatever you do, you are ordained to do it. If you drive a delivery truck, you're an ordained delivery-man, helping to lubricate the wheels of commerce to bring essential supplies to your customers. If you are a farmer, you're an ordained farmer, growing crops that parents need to feed their children. If you are a landscape worker, you're an ordained landscape worker, creating and maintaining beauty that soothes weary souls at the end of a long workday. If you are... well, you get the idea.

> ■ ■ ■
>
> "I'm an ordained
> math teacher."
>
> ■ ■ ■

That's right, you don't have to go into full-time ministry to make a mark.

Every vocation is holy to God. As theologian Francis Schaeffer wrote, "A ministry such as teaching the Bible in a college is no higher calling intrinsically than being a business-man or doing something else."

Your work is not merely a platform to serve God. It *is* serving God. The work itself is important to God. The apostle Paul expressed it this way:

> Whatever you do, work at it with all your heart, as
> working for the Lord, not for men.... It is the Lord
> Christ you are serving. (Colossians 3:23–24, NIV)

You don't just fix computers all day to give you the money to do what's *really* important. Fixing computers *is* really important. Or fixing cars, plumbing, or teeth—all types of fixing I needed while writing this book.

What have you been ordained to do?

One area of real confusion for a lot of men is whether they should go into full-time ministry once they get really turned on to Jesus. But that's rarely the case. The advice of Paul is that "each of you should remain as you were when God called you" (1 Corinthians 7:20). In roughly 99 percent of cases, I'd estimate, God wants men right where they are but with a whole new motivation.

Ryan's pastor poured himself into Ryan and his family. Spiritually, Ryan grew rapidly, and soon he wanted to serve

God. He started teaching a class to parents with young children. That was like pouring accelerant on the fire. Ryan said, "That was the highest growth I've ever experienced. The impact on my whole family was profound."

Ryan assumed that the next step for his growth was to go into full-time ministry. So he did. But he soon began to miss the project management role he'd had in a corporate environment. He was bummed that he didn't feel any special glow because he was in vocational ministry. In fact, he felt less alive and significant than before.

The ministry organization where he worked helped Ryan understand what you've just read—that every vocation is holy, that for a Christian there is no such thing as a secular job.

He realized that project management was his calling. He had a unique talent to lead teams and meet deadlines. Plus, in his previous job, he'd had opportunities to evangelistically share his faith—something he couldn't do with all-Christian coworkers. Ryan was ecstatic when his former employer welcomed him back with open arms.

"Ironically, working in a ministry stalled my growth," he told me. "It has taken a while for me to recover. Recently, I've committed to teach the Bible again. I've missed the growth."

Most of us don't need to do something else. We just need to do what we're already called to do, but with the fresh perspective that everything we do can be done for the glory of God.

Do you have the gift of speaking? Then speak as though God himself were speaking through you. Do you have the gift of helping others? Do it with all the strength and energy that God supplies. Then everything you do will bring glory to God through Jesus Christ. All glory and power to him forever and ever! Amen. (1 Peter 4:11)

You can be utterly confident that even the most common tasks have lasting significance when done for the glory of God.

Where would you like to make a difference? Is it through business, art, education, the building trades, science, the service sector, the military? Well, whatever it is that gets your adrenaline pumping, the Creation Mandate is your permission slip. Go for it! It's the horizontal part of your mission, and it's what you were created to do.

BUILDING CHRIST'S KINGDOM

The second key that unlocks significance for a man is tasks that relate to our vertical life. For we who ache for our lives to count for eternal things, Jesus issued the purest distillation ever uttered of how we can accomplish that:

I have been given all authority in heaven and on earth. Therefore, go and make disciples of all the nations,

baptizing them in the name of the Father and the Son
and the Holy Spirit. Teach these new disciples to obey
all the commands I have given you. And be sure of
this: I am with you always, even to the end of the age.
(Matthew 28:18–20)

Whew! It's all there! Inspiration. Challenge. Authority. Adventure. Mission. Focus. A personal invitation to a life that counts forever.

These are the final marching orders of Jesus. They've never been amended, altered, or rescinded. It is our mission. And it is great. That's why we call it the Great Commission.

The Great Commission includes everything and anything that leads people to Jesus in faith and repentance (call), prepares them to grow in spiritual maturity and wisdom (equip), and motivates them to love and good deeds (send).

In plain words: pass it on.

God loves to use us to help other people find Jesus.

NUDGING OTHERS TOWARD JESUS

Passing it on usually happens best when it's part of our everyday encounters. Watch the Great Commission at work in the following everyday encounters.

One day I went to a favorite garden center. It was a warm

day, and noticing my warm-up suit, the twenty-something clerk struck up a conversation. "I'll bet you're hot in that outfit," she said.

"Well, it is a little warm," I said. "How about you? You work in this heat all day?" (She wanted to talk about the weather, so I talked to her about the weather.)

"You don't know the half of it," she began. "I just moved back from Vermont, and I'm having a tough time adjusting to the Florida heat."

"What were you doing in Vermont?" I asked.

"Actually, I had to get away to try and find myself," she offered.

"So how did you do?"

"To be honest, I'm still pretty confused. My father is from India, my mother is a nominal Catholic, and my brother is a Baptist who keeps telling me that if I don't accept Jesus I'm going to hell. I've been studying world religions, and I think there are many ways to God. What do you think?"

"Actually, you're probably asking the wrong person," I said. "You see, I'm what you might call a born-again Christian. In other words, I have put my faith exclusively in Jesus Christ to forgive my sins and give me eternal life. But it does bother me that your brother would say that. I guess that's not a very compelling argument for you, is it?"

"No," she agreed, "it's not."

"Listen, Amy," I continued. "Your brother is, basically, talking like a nut. Even if he's right, that's no way to talk. Let me suggest a couple of things. First, if you go to the tomb of Confucius, you will find it's occupied. If you go to the tomb of Buddha, it's occupied. If you go to the tomb of Muhammad, it's also occupied. But if you go to the tomb of Jesus, it's empty. That intrigues me, Amy, and it should intrigue you too." (She wanted to talk comparative religion, so I just followed the conversation.)

> ▪ ▪ ▪
>
> "Jesus is the only one of those four men who claimed to be God."
>
> ▪ ▪ ▪

"Jesus is the only one of those four men who claimed to be God. If that's true, then don't you think you owe it to yourself to find that out?" (Notice that I was now recommending Jesus.)

"Yeah, but there's no way to know for sure," she offered.

"Actually there is," I suggested. "Do you have a Bible?"

"Oh yes," she said. "My brother gave me a big, thick Bible." (And then I invited her to take a simple action step—to check out the claims of Christ for herself.)

"Okay, then. Let me make a suggestion. Is that all right?" She nodded, so I continued. "In the Bible there is a short book called the gospel of John. It contains twenty-one very short chapters—about thirty pages altogether. Why don't you investigate the claims of Jesus for yourself? You could read a chapter a day for three weeks. John recorded some of Christ's most remarkable words in those few pages. I would also suggest you pray something like 'Jesus, if You are God, then reveal Yourself to me in these pages.'

"Frankly, Amy, I can't do any better. If Jesus is who He says, then He doesn't need me to argue His case. You can decide for yourself. What do you think?"

"You know, I think I'll do that," she said with obvious sincerity. And my part was done.

Evangelism is simply taking someone as far as he or she wants to go toward Jesus. In Amy's case, that was as far as we could go—she was at work, after all. So I prayed for her as I drove away, knowing that I had been faithful and trusting that God would send her exactly the right person to help her take exactly the next right step at exactly the right time.

You cannot scientifically prove the existence of God, but you don't have to. By all means, share what Jesus has meant to you. But then let Jesus speak for Himself. If the story of Jesus, once understood, doesn't draw people into a transforming encounter with God, nothing you add will draw them either. Our job is to be faithful, not to produce a particular result.

Here's another example. Jeff helped the Sony Corporation develop its webcasting technology. He traveled around the country webcasting Foo Fighters concerts and the Easter egg hunt on the White House lawn. He definitely felt like he was making a difference horizontally in the temporal world. But he also saw lots of vertical potential for the eternal world, so he began praying, "God, how can we use this technology to help build Your kingdom?"

One day in 2000, Jeff approached me and said, "What would you think if I started webcasting the Friday morning Bible studies?"

"Sure, sounds great!" I said. "What's webcasting?" (Remember, YouTube didn't come along until 2005.)

Today those webcasts go out weekly to all fifty states and dozens of countries around the world—all because Jeff wanted to make a difference for God.

> ■ ■ ■
>
> Our job is to be faithful, not to produce a particular result.
>
> ■ ■ ■

One more. Jack was a Christian, but he ran his business like the good times would never end. When the great recession of 2008 hit, he couldn't see any way out. With a chilling resolve, he told his friend Jamal, "I've got a $1 million life insurance policy. I've decided that the best thing for everybody would be for me to commit suicide."

Jamal wanted to make a difference for God in Jack's life. Jamal had a strong conviction about passing on what he had received because of something the apostle Paul wrote: "You have heard me teach things that have been confirmed by many reliable witnesses. Now teach these truths to other trustworthy people who will be able to pass them on to others" (2 Timothy 2:2).

So Jamal helped Jack develop a short-term plan to stabilize his financial situation. This included finding any kind of job to show good faith to his terrified wife. Jack's hope returned rapidly. God worked in his life, and his dormant love for spiritual things came back stronger than ever.

Next, it was Jack's turn to pass it on. Jack started meeting with another man, Graham, who was in the same boat. Jack e-mailed me this: "I met with Graham last week and tried to help him with a possible part-time job like mine, but he left me a voicemail today and said nothing was available. He sounded down, so I am going to call him after sending you this e-mail."

Jack reluctantly gave permission to use his story, not because he was embarrassed, but because, as he said, he doesn't see himself as a good example. I disagree.

What Jack did is exactly what Jesus had in mind. He made a difference. And so can you.

Remember, God prepared your program of service before you were even a seed in the loins of your earthly father. It doesn't get any more primal than that! And now that you've seen that everything is spiritual, both the vertical and the horizontal tasks, you can map out a personal mission statement that will help you satisfy your primal need for significance.

Here's a work sheet you can use to chart your course.

YOUR PERSONAL LIFE MISSION STATEMENT WORK SHEET

God has wired you to make a difference and leave the world a better place. I invite you to thoughtfully map out a personal mission statement that will help you satisfy your primal need for significance. Use a separate sheet of paper to write your answers, where applicable.

1. *Begin with prayer,* asking God to give you wisdom, clarity, and closure.

2. *Write down verses of Scripture* that have a special meaning for you.

3. *Identify your gifts.* God gives each of us spiritual gifts. You will find them listed in four passages of Scripture:
   - Romans 12:6–8
   - 1 Corinthians 12:4–11
   - Ephesians 4:11–13
   - 1 Peter 4:10–11.

   What are your gifts? (Write them down.)

4. *Be patient.* You may be gung-ho to get this all down on paper, but it could take several days, weeks, or even months if you're new to this kind of thinking. If it takes longer, ask God what He wants to build into, or remove from, your life during the wait.

5. *Complete these statements* for what will make you feel fully alive.

   ■ What I think I have been ordained to do for the glory of God is...

   ■ *The Creation Mandate:* What will make me feel most significant, most alive, and most useful in the horizontal world of my family, work, and community is...

   ■ *The Great Commission:* What will make me feel most significant, most alive, and most useful in the vertical world of making disciples is...

■ ■ ■

PUTTING IT
ALL TOGETHER

As a young executive in a Fortune 500 company, Jim (a different Jim than the Jim whose son died of AIDS) was fast-tracked
for leadership development. He quickly shot up the company
ladder, and within ten years the senior execs started grooming
Jim for a top management position.

In the meantime, a lot was going on in Jim's personal life
too. In his twenties, Jim fell madly in love with Thelma. They
married and had four children. Jim loved those kids so much.
But his ever-increasing work load eventually had him leaving
home before his children got up and getting home after they
had gone to bed.

Jim loved his job, but he loved his family more. He also saw
how the long hours were destroying the personal lives of other
execs. After much soul searching, prayer, advice seeking, and
talking it over with Thelma, Jim decided to cap his career. He
started turning down promotions. Eventually he found a position that still scratched his itch to do significant work but also
allowed him to lead a more balanced life.

Once he was able to start keeping normal work hours, Jim's
whole world changed. He poured himself into his kids. He
found time to serve around his church. He offered leadership to

a local urban youth ministry. He led a group of men as a table leader at our Bible study for fifteen years.

Not long ago, Jim and Thelma celebrated their fiftieth anniversary with a dinner attended by all their children and their spouses, their pastor, and forty friends, including Patsy and me. Their pastor gave a moving tribute about the many lives Jim had touched.

As we drove home that night, I thought about how Jim—a generation older than me—had made his mark and what lessons his life had to offer. After all those years, it boiled down to this: Jim had an eternal relationship with God, a happy wife, Christian children who still wanted to be around him, a job where he made a contribution, scores of lives he impacted for Jesus, a pastor willing to say something nice about him, and forty loving friends.

I asked myself, *What more could a man want that really matters?*

God has wired each of us—you, me, and every other man—with a deeply felt need to be significant and to feel like our lives are going somewhere. Nothing feels quite as good as coming to the end of a long day—or a long life—like an exhausted warrior, knowing that you have spent yourself in a worthy cause for the glory of God.

This is what it feels like to be a man alive!

REFLECTION AND DISCUSSION QUESTIONS

1   What is your dream to make a difference, spend yourself in a worthy cause, and leave the world a better place?

2   In this chapter we saw that everything is spiritual—both the *vertical* tasks of the Great Commission and the *horizontal* tasks of the Creation Mandate. What do you need to rethink about the way you approach finding significance?

3   To the best of your ability to understand it at this point, what is God's program of service for you? What did you learn by completing "Your Personal Life Mission Statement" work sheet? Where are you confident in your responses? Where are your thoughts still developing? What do you want to do differently as a result of this chapter and your group discussion?

AFTERWORD

What do you suppose Welles Crowther was thinking when he paused on the stairwell that day in Lower Manhattan, then turned around and headed back up into the smoke and destruction of the South Tower?

Of course, no one can possibly know for sure. But I want to hazard a guess. Because I think I know.

I wonder if you do too.

As we've seen throughout this book, every man is directed by deep, instinctive needs that we often barely understand and that never go away. We've called them primal needs, and they are God created. These powerful needs exist somewhere before words and beyond choice.

That's why I don't believe Welles was thinking very much that morning. I don't honestly believe he was weighing his options, covering his bases, looking for a win or a way out. Do you?

I think, in those frantic moments, he was simply rising up to seize with all his might nothing less than Welles Crowther fully alive—the guy in the red bandana, God's one-of-a-kind masterpiece He planned long ago.

Are you still with me?

Stories like the one about Welles stir something deep inside men for a reason. It kills us to just go through the motions. I keep a sentence at the top of my to-do list that says, "I would rather die for a worthy cause than live for no reason."

Thankfully, not many of us will be called on to literally lay down our lives. Nevertheless, you and I have been called to die, to be dead to self and alive to Christ. That's why Paul said, "I have been crucified with Christ and I no longer live, but Christ lives in me. The life I live in the body, I live by faith in the Son of God, who loved me and gave himself for me" (Galatians 2:20, NIV).

We are no longer our own. We have been bought with a price and saved for a purpose—to live each day in the trans-forming power of Christ alive in us.

So here's your challenge. Instead of ignoring your primal needs, or letting them drag you into a wasted life, claim them as God's gifts to you. Allow Him to transform the restless en-ergy you feel into a powerful spiritual life.

If He can die for us, the least we can do is live for Him.

That's what it means to be a man alive. Let's go get it!

DISCUSSION
LEADERS GUIDE

Y ou can start a group to discuss *Man Alive* and lead a lively discussion by following these guidelines:

1. *Plan on meeting for eight weeks—one week for each chapter in the book.* Your group may be an existing Bible study, fellowship group, prayer group, or adult education class (women can be included). Or you may want to start a new group.

2. *How to start a new group.* Photocopy the contents and the questions at the end of a couple of chapters, and give copies of these to the men you want to meet with. Ask them if they would like to be in a discussion group that would read the book and answer the discussion questions at the end of each chapter. This can be a group from work, church, your neighborhood, or a combination. The optimum group size is from eight to twelve men (assuming some men will have to miss a week occasionally). If the group gels, you may want

to suggest that the group continue to meet after you are finished studying *Man Alive*.

3. *Distribute a copy of the book to each member.* Identify the first chapter as the reading assignment for your first meeting, and ask the group members to be prepared to answer the questions at the end of the chapter. The questions at the end of chapter 1 are designed to break the ice and get men talking. Close with a prayer. Always adjourn on time.

4. *Suggested meeting format.* Begin with an icebreaker question, such as, "Anyone have a particularly good or tough week?" Or you can purchase the DVD series with eight short sessions designed to reactivate the material and set up the questions. For a one-hour meeting, a good schedule to follow would be the following:

- ■ Discuss icebreaker question or view a *Man Alive* DVD (five minutes).
- ■ Discuss the questions at the end of the chapter (forty-five minutes).
- ■ Pray as a group (ten minutes).

5. *Have coffee and soft drinks available.* If you meet over breakfast or lunch, allow an extra twenty minutes for eating, if possible.

6. *Leading a discussion.* The key to a successful discussion group is your ability to ensure that each member gets airtime. Your role is to encourage each man to share his thoughts and ideas on the weekly chapter. If a group member asks an off-the-subject question, simply suggest that you discuss that issue at a separate time. If someone rambles too much, privately ask him to help you draw out the more shy members of the group. Take each question in order, and make sure everyone has the opportunity to comment. If you have a shy member, take the initiative and address him by name—for example, "John, how would you answer question 3?"

7. You don't have to be an experienced Bible teacher to lead a discussion about *Man Alive.* If someone asks you a question beyond your scope, simply say so and move on. Your role is to facilitate a discussion, not teach the group.

8. Check out additional resources, such as the article "How to Lead a Weekly Men's Small Group" at ManAliveBook.com.

Send me an e-mail at patrickmorley@maninthemirror.org to let me know how it goes or to ask questions.

ACKNOWLEDGMENTS

Taking a book to market is a labor of love and ten thousand details. It takes a team.

As always, my amazing wife, Patsy, acted as my sounding board, offering both encouragement and wisdom. Thank you for your unconditional love and acceptance.

My only literary agent for my entire career has been Robert Wolgemuth and his agency, Wolgemuth & Associates Inc. Thank you, Robert, Eric, and Andrew Wolgemuth, my literary agents and friends, for always knowing the next right step.

I'm deeply indebted to the entire WaterBrook Multnomah team. My special thanks to Ken Petersen and David Kopp for embracing me as a men's author and catching the vision for this book to inspire and challenge men to lead powerful lives transformed by Jesus. Dave, you summoned your editorial genius to pull a book out of me that I wasn't sure was possible. I believe God put us together to reach deep into men's stagnant lives. I'll be forever grateful. I would also like to thank you, Carie Freimuth and Lori Addicott, and the stellar teams you oversee, for bringing such energy and creativity to this project. I can't believe how invested you get into your authors. I thank God for you. Steve Reed, thank you for your long-time friendship and partnership with Man in the Mirror's Books by the Box! ministry to churches. Allison O'Hara, you have been my champion since day one. They told me you were a rainmaker. Now I know why. Thank you Ashley Boyer for your diligence on my behalf to get the word out. Kris Orr, I'm in awe of your perseverance to find just the right cover design. Chris Sigfrids, I'm so grateful for your help to integrate media and technology into this project. Thanks, Sara Selkirk, for shepherding the book to the general market. And thank you, Laura Wright, for managing all the production details, and for making such a confusing process seem like a walk in the park. Because of you all, I'm utterly convinced that every leader, pastor, and man who needs to know about this book will know.

Eric Stanford, you did a stellar job line editing the manuscript. You have the gift. Thank you.

Special thanks also go to Scott Crossman and his Thursday morning Bible study for pilot testing the book in a small-group format.

Jon Thurman, John Morley, Daryl Carter, Ruthie Delk, and Jen Simmons served as early manuscript readers and gave highly useful feedback that ultimately altered my direction. Thanks for saving me!

Special thanks go to Bill Helms and John Morley, who

reviewed the final manuscript and made some catches that would have left me with egg on my face. John Morley, your eye for logic and coherency are amazing! I'm so proud of you!

James Spradlin deserves special recognition for all the hours he invested in helping me figure out the creative direction for the DVD series that goes with the book. Special kudos to Jon Strong and Brent Buffington for the immense creativity and energy they brought to writing, filming, and producing the DVDs.

Kevin McMillan, your work on the ManAliveBook.com website and cover proves once again that you are a master craftsman.

A special word of thanks to our dedicated headquarters staff at Man in the Mirror. They've heard everything in this book and helped sharpen the concepts over the years: Jim Angelakos, Sharon Carey, Brett Clemmer, David Delk, Al Lenio, Stephanie Lopez, Michael Maine, Scott Russell, Tracie Searles, Jim Seibert, Jamie Turco, and Rise Wilson, but especially to Ruth Cameron, my trusted executive assistant. Thank you.

NOTES

8 80 percent of men are so emotionally impaired, Terrence Real, *I Don't Want to Talk About It* (New York: Fireside, 1997), 146.

8 55 percent of marriages, Howard Dayton, personal correspondence with the author, October 22, 2011.

8 50 percent of men who attend church, "Pornography Statistics," Family Safe Media, www.familysafemedia .com/pornography_statistics.html. I once spoke at a Christian meeting of five hundred men who were asked if they had actively sought out pornography within the previous year. Approximately 60 percent of the men wrote *yes* on a slip of paper and dropped it into a basket on their way to a break.

8 40 percent of men get divorced, American Academy of Pediatrics, "Family Pediatrics Report of the Task Force on the Family," *Pediatrics* 111, no. 6 (2003): 1541–71.

8 one-third of America's seventy-two million children, US Census Bureau, "Living Arrangements of Children," April 1996.

45 unlike women, men tend to deny, Terrence Real, *I Don't Want to Talk About It* (New York: Fireside, 1997), p. 56.

95 biblical counseling must insist, Larry Crabb, foreword to *The Wounded Heart,* by Dan B. Allender (Colorado Springs, CO: NavPress, 1990).

111 The Barna Group's "State of the Church" report, Barna Group, "20 Years of Surveys Show Key Differences in the Faith of America's Men and Women," State of the Church Series, 2011, Part 3: Gender Differences, August 1, 2011, www.barna.org/faith-spirituality/508-20-years -of-surveys-show-key-differences-in-the-faith-of-americas -men-and-women.

145 Not long ago I wrote a book, Patrick Morley and David Delk, *The Marriage Prayer* (Chicago: Moody, 2008). You can find a printable copy of his and her versions at ManAliveBook.com, under "The Marriage Prayer."

ABOUT THE AUTHOR

For decades Patrick Morley has been regarded as one of America's most respected authorities on the unique challenges and opportunities that men face. Through his speaking and writing he is a tireless advocate for men, encouraging and inspiring them to change their lives in Christ.

In 1973, Patrick founded Morley Properties, which, for several years, was hailed as one of Florida's one hundred largest privately held companies. During this time he was the president or managing partner of fifty-nine companies and partnerships.

In 1989, he wrote *The Man in the Mirror,* a landmark book rooted in his own search for purpose and a deeper relationship with God. With over three million copies in print, *The Man in the Mirror* captured the imaginations of men worldwide and was selected as one of the hundred most influential Christian books of the twentieth century. Altogether, Patrick has written eighteen books and more than five hundred articles. He has appeared on several hundred radio and television programs.

In 1991, Patrick founded Man in the Mirror, a ministry that has impacted the lives of ten million men worldwide, distributed nine million books, and last year worked with thirty thousand church leaders to more effectively disciple men. He speaks to men daily through *The Man in the Mirror* radio program, which is carried on three hundred stations nationwide.

In addition, Patrick teaches a Bible study every Friday morning to approximately 5,000 men—150 men live in Orlando, Florida, and he reaches the others through a Bible study webcast over the Internet in all fifty states and throughout the world.

"The ministry of Man in the Mirror exists," says Patrick Morley, "in answer to the prayers of all those wives, mothers, and grandmothers who have for decades been praying for the men in their lives."

Patrick Morley graduated with honors from the University of Central Florida. He has earned a PhD in management, completed postgraduate studies at the Harvard Business School and Oxford University, and graduated from Reformed Theological Seminary. He lives in Winter Park, Florida, with his wife, Patsy. They have two married children and four grandchildren.

His weekly Video Bible Study, articles, books, and e-books can be found at ManInTheMirror.org, and you can follow him on Facebook at www.facebook.com/PatrickMorleyAuthor and on Twitter @patrickmorley.

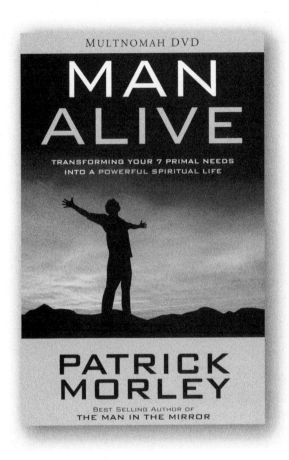

In this 8-week DVD Study Resource based on the core book, Patrick Morley uses an informal setting interwoven with video clips to discuss the key insights of *Man Alive* and lead viewers in an interactive learning experience. Suitable for personal or group use.

In this "quick-start" overview of *Man Alive*, Patrick Morley shares the poignant story of his struggle to reconcile with his father and emphasizes how embracing God's unconditional love brought him the freedom and healing he was looking for. Available in packs of 10, ideal for churches, small group distribution, and men's outreach ministries.

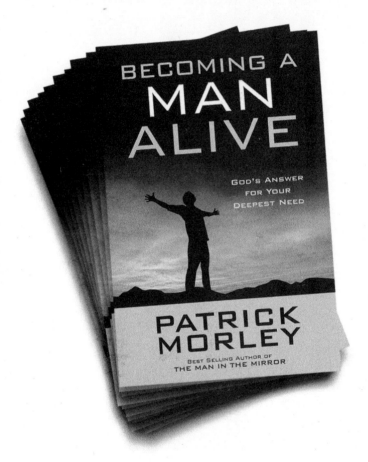

Additional resources available at
ManAliveBook.com